ISBN: 978-0-9964265-6-5

Ron Paul Institute
FOR PEACE AND PROSPERITY
WWW.RONPAULINSTITUTE.ORG
833 W. Plantation Dr. ◆ Clute, TX 77531

The Great Surreptitious Coup
Who Stole Western Civilization?

by
RON PAUL

Nihilism vs. A 'Higher Law'

Liberals and Conservatives alike have adapted to the "Coup." Even though, with different explanations and goals, both groups, along with many others, have been participants in the most successful coup in human history. Western Civilization is being threatened, while the US political system that John Locke and Thomas Jefferson devised is now in a comatose state. This has been aided and abetted by a gross distortion of truth. The inexorable growth of government authoritarianism in the past century has produced a horrendous crisis that is destined to be a lot more dangerous than the Great Depression and WW II.

Conservatives, who for decades have accepted "modest "attacks on liberty because they were always associated with promises that the benefits — couched in patriotic terms — made more government and less freedom seem tolerable. Various factors for many years made the transition away from liberty and toward intrusive government seem less painful under the influence of powerful lobbyists who could provide the political, financial, and "moral" cover to those who benefitted from the compromise.

The "Great Coup" would have never been possible without the authoritarians who worked with the politicians and the Deep State cabal to get their allies placed in key strategic positions throughout the political-economic and social system. Many well-informed individuals are convinced that billionaires sympathetic to modern-day fascism provided the finances to achieve this amazing success in infiltrating the judicial system, the educational system, the social media, the mainstream media, and politics at all levels. Together these infiltrated sectors have promoted the Covid lockdown policies, our constant wars, and especially the monopoly control of the world financial system by the Federal Reserve.

They have not been bashful about their enthusiasm for the goals and tactics of "Wokeism." Getting the business community to willingly become the enforcement arm of government to institutionalize the Covid-era mandates was astounding. The policy of censoring and "canceling" citizens is characteristic of a dictatorship, not of a free society. This shift in attitude and the capitulation to supporting the infiltration of a strong fascist ideology into our everyday activities has been a shocking eye-opener. The big question is: "How did we get so far removed from the principles of liberty that were once crucial to America's greatness?"

In the beginning, proponents of strictly limiting government power were easily persuaded to "tweak" the system if business, banking, and the military-industrial complex were to benefit from tax code changes, Federal Reserve monetary inflation, and other goodies like contracts, subsidies, and favorable regulations — from which all citizens could at times benefit.

Over the many decades, our college professors have taught generations of conservatives, liberals, and all other beneficiaries of government's "free stuff," that "deficits don't matter." More people are now recognizing that it's just another government lie and that inflated food and gasoline prices are revealing the truth that "deficits do matter".

Going to war for "national security" reasons and protecting our empire's vital interests became the battle cry for a large majority of Americans, lest their patriotism be challenged. Our wealth and power were deemed to be unchallengeable. It was never a giant leap for the "conservative" business and banking interests to join the liberal big spenders in aligning themselves with a government-run economic system that controlled the distribution of wealth stollen from the middle class. A form of corporatism has always been a convenient alternative to accepting actual fascism. But today, supporters of fascism and Cultural Marxism have made tremendous inroads with their systematic attacks on liberty and the free market.

This liberal/conservative Deep State Cabal has conspired to "cancel" the ideas crucial to understanding the principles of liberty. These views had been well received during the period of the Enlightenment between 1685 and 1815. It was these ideas that changed the world for the better by contributing greatly to the magnificence of Western Civilization and the uniqueness of America's founding. The current struggle today is between those who are determined to "cancel" Western Civilization, end the already diminished American Republic, and acquiesce to Marxist propaganda and principles.

However, there are others who prefer to seize upon this opportunity to advance the understanding of how a free society provides the greatest abundance for all and the best chance to live in a more peaceful world. The difference in benefits offered by the two options should be self-evident. Yet authoritarians along with pretend Constitutionalists together make similar grandiose promises regarding the issue of liberty for the masses. Arguments among these two groups for years have raged on over the proper role of government in mankind's effort to devise the best system for securing these benefits — all while pretending that thirst for political power is not their real motive.

In 1776 America staked out a unique political system designed by Thomas Jefferson and incorporating the wisdom of John Locke, along with the accumulated knowledge over the millennia, that acknowledged an awareness of a "higher law," and the principle of "natural law."

It's been a long trek from the time of "Adam and Eve" to America's founding and now to the point where today many Americans are worrying about being "canceled" from society for the "crime" of merely mentioning the need to seek the truth of a "higher law." The danger of ignoring the futility of nihilism was acknowledged in the "Garden of Eden" allegory. This early profound discovery of this great conundrum of deciding "right from wrong" institutionalized a universal challenge to be dealt with by all mankind. The "good versus evil" issue will never lie dormant. Nor will it be resolved in the world we know today. But it will be well worth it for all people to participate in the search for an honest understanding of this moral imperative.

Currently, worldwide, we find the corollary "nihilism," is on the march and at times appears insurmountable. The rejection of the existence of objective truth, when accepted by the politicians, is a grave danger to the people's liberty.

The modern-day philosophic quagmire in which we find ourselves has led many people to choose the false promises and violence of authoritarianism in their search for happiness and meaning in their lives. In the short term, a "bonus" of material benefits flows into the pockets of those obedient to the ultimate goals and directives of today's Cultural Marxists. Man's effort to maintain a moral compass with the "higher law" in hibernation will cause many to yield to the temptation of evil over virtue, thus allowing evil to thrive.

Good vs evil has been with us ever since mankind could reasonably record and reflect on the intense desire to comprehend man's purpose on earth. The *sine qua non* of this search has been a persistent desire to clearly define right and wrong and decide exactly who or what principles should provide the guiding light for man's peaceful existence. The story of Adam and Eve did not provide a precise political answer to this profound question. Instead, the nature of the inquiry emphasized the necessity to constantly seek wisdom and a desire to confront the issue of right and wrong.

If one believes that harmony and peace are worthy goals for the human condition, recognizing the principle of a higher law and confronting the issue of right and wrong are crucial.

The pervasive corruption of today's society has precipitated many serious discussions regarding the future of Western Civilization and even its possible demise. In dealing with this gargantuan problem one must first consider the nature and origin of "Western Civilization." If the moral challenge of deciding the difference between right and wrong and acting accordingly is rejected by the people, all TRUST is lost and civility becomes a rare and fragile social "commodity." Without this understanding, civilizations do not advance nor are they maintained. The greater the hostility toward a "higher law" principle, the greater becomes its need.

The spiritual void that results from rejection of a "higher law" principle leads to the view that arguing over "right and wrong" is useless and the only logical substitute therefore becomes nihilism. In America today that's what all the fuss is about. The nihilists will not rest until the belief in a higher law is vanquished and authoritarian "wisdom" and aggressive power prevail, unhampered in all matters, at the expense of the liberty that took thousands of years to — imperfectly — establish a progressive civilization. This trend need not be blindly accepted as a "dead letter," but for civilization's sake certain principles of Western Culture must be restored.

The origin of Western Civilization

Western Civilization is under attack. This has been the most significant period of time in all recorded history documenting the greatest advancements of the human race in knowledge, prosperity and technology. Unfortunately, it has also been a time of the unimaginable carnage of human beings applying modern technology to kill each other in constant war. This in spite of the advancement of spirituality throughout the ages by many religions that recognized that the constant killing did not represent good behavior designed by a higher law.

Still, the advancement in what has become commonly known as Western Civilization has continued to technologically progress, far surpassing the wildest imaginations just a short time ago. It was humbling to me to have heard stories from my dad about delivering milk to retail customers in a horse and wagon in the early 20th century!

Western Civilization may have lost a bit of its early grandeur but its momentum in economic creativity, for now, remains impressive. Unfortunately, this is now being accomplished by consuming previously earned wealth and incurring massive debt instead of current production. In the meantime, cultural and ethical standards have turned regressive as a consequence of the government-run educational system and deteriorating social and moral standards. One should expect the same decline in economic and technological achievements from these cultural changes that are now controlled by the radical Progressives, now to be found as leaders of the destructive "Wokeism" cult.

The development of Western Civilization was not a mere coincidence or an act of nature. It resulted from thoughtful creative human beings who had been given intelligence and an incentive to participate in this solemn pursuit of truth in order to improve the human condition. Western Civilization, though far from perfect, when compared to all other similar periods in history, was found far superior.

But what does the future hold for these past great contributions to Western Civilization? The evidence is growing that they are under attack at their very roots. Does this mean that advancement of civilization will remain stagnant in a moral and philosophic new dark age? Or will the effort for advancement self-destruct? Doubts are growing that it will "catch its breath" and then resume economic and cultural advancement, guided by a higher law principle, in an effort to move the world toward a more peaceful and prosperous society.

If more leaders choose guidance from natural law, the "higher law" of nature, in preference to succumbing to the moral bankruptcy of the aggressive nihilistic cult of "Wokeist" authoritarians, I'm convinced it can make a difference in the ongoing effort to improve the human condition for centuries to come. If the known benefits of Western Civilization that have developed over the millennia are "canceled," humanity will face unfathomable consequences. The remnant needs a greater awakening to energize a new generation just now discovering the tremendous benefits of a liberty-driven society.

Though many are predicting that the world is facing horrendous results from a society that rejects the "higher law" principle and is replacing it with an immoral nihilistic belief system, it is not my contention that the disasters are inevitable. Human behavior makes a difference. The only real question to be decided is whether people will retain enough liberty to overcome the near total nonsense and lies that have infiltrated the world's social, cultural, economic, and political order — lies that continue to smother every effort to promote natural law and a standard of morality compatible with the higher law principle.

The higher law principle — from the beginning of time

The "higher law" is the consequence of man's effort, from the beginning of time, to seek the plain truth of all things relating to the difference between "right and wrong." It has been said that parents and other authorities imprint this wisdom into the conscience of the young in the early stages of intellectual development. Thereafter, it is expected that each one then will theoretically know right from wrong.

This is true to a certain degree. Parents and others are indeed instrumental in giving innocent children a moral compass for guidance in all inter-related social activities. Even if a child is denied this teaching at home, it has been generally accepted that most people come to know the difference between good and evil and that knowledge is readily available to all who seek truth. The great challenge for all individuals is to understand that we ultimately have an obligation to make our own moral choices.

The debate has frequently been: Do we have "free will" to assume responsibility for making these decisions or are we automatons willing to be dictated to by authoritarians claiming that only they know what is best for us and society? Obedience to a "higher law" is far superior to avoiding the challenge of seeking the truth for guidance in our personal moral behavior.

The opposite of accepting this responsibility is to

accept the premise that truth is not available to us —
as nihilism claims. One must then also believe there is
no evidence that the principle of "good and evil" exists either. Anything goes! Seeking virtue, for many, is
a waste of time. For a demonstration of this one only
needs to visit our inner cities, many of which are now
run by individuals who outrightly reject the "higher law"
and believe they have the power and moral authority to
arbitrarily write the rules for their own benefit, without
consequence, as they go along.

Recently, thousands of American "recruits" were
trained in this authoritarian approach to controlling
society by adapting to Marxism with a cultural twist.
The man-made Covid epidemic was the excuse for the
"show and tell" demonstration on how nihilistic beliefs
can be imposed on gullible citizens in order to "cancel"
the influence of the higher law. The cult of Wokeism is a
consequence of the influence this approach has gained at
the expense of respect for natural law. This is a significant
departure from the moral and economic standards en-
couraged by the US Constitution, the non-aggression principle, and Christianity. Purposely promoting social discord
is the only logical explanation for the current foolish and
dangerous economic and social policies challenging Western culture. This is a goal that the proponents have readily
admitted to.

Liberty and truth for nihilists are empty words
without meaning and are absent from their vocabulary.
Hypocrisy and demagoguery have become convenient tools
for the politicians void of any instinct for virtue as they
promote a pretense of caring for the people's welfare. If

they deny that "truth" exists, but pretend to tell the truth, it has no value and causes great harm.

We should expect this conflict, between nihilism and the principles of a higher law to continue indefinitely if the history of mankind over the past 5,000 years gives us a hint as to the future of Western Civilization.

Early great contributions to Western Civilization?

The uniqueness of Western Civilization has allowed for tremendous cultural and economic advancement with unbelievable progress in most human endeavors. It has been conceded by most historians that the influences from both Roman and Greek civilizations have played a significant role in the early development of Western culture.

As important as these contributions have been, even prior to the Greek and Roman period there were many other cultures that assisted in the inexorable march of the human race toward the marvels of Western Civilization. There was little evidence during the squalor of prehistoric times of the magnificence that has since been generated during the Enlightenment period and the subsequent development of Western Civilization. History has been able to record a lot of what has transpired in the last 5,000 years as Western culture grew in stature and influence.

The influence of the earlier Civilizations of Ancient Egypt and Mesopotamia all shared in building the foundation upon which the unique and startling progress of Western Civilization was built. There is no "day one," *per se*, for exactly when Western Civilization began. "Day one," in many ways, actually began when the first language was developed and the first book was written which has facilitated recording historic events for the benefit future generations. Language development and record-keeping stimulated in some intellectual curiosity and reflection on the past, while others were prompted to contemplate and reason about an enticing future.

Human communications require these two important features: reflection to understand the past and reason to plan for the future. Many intellectual tools, along with the accumulated knowledge of the past, have assisted in the steady development of what has become known as Western Civilization. With these tools available, the ability to pass on knowledge about past social, political, military, economic, agricultural, ethical, and religious values was greatly enhanced.

There are no precise dates for when language became a useful tool in aiding the natural development of civilization. Most people, though, concede that human progress would have been impossible without the ability to communicate with others about past, present, and possible future events through use of language.

The first written Language probably originated in ancient Sumeria, 3,400 years BC or 5600 years ago. The Greek contributions to advancing civilization were recognized early on and were immense. The early Greek philosophers developed a reputation for pursuing truth in their effort to achieve progress. Socrates, Aristotle, and Plato were giants in the march toward an advanced civilization. Our recent failed efforts in dealing with the Covid crisis could have benefited greatly with a good dose of ancient Greek wisdom, emphasizing reason, truth, and equal justice.

The Romans followed up by maintaining the cultural and scientific advancements of the Greeks while making their own significant contributions toward the advancement of Western Civilization. They were instrumental in emphasizing individual rights when writing laws, arguing that they be equally fair to both the rich and poor. The Romans revolutionized civil engineering while constructing roads, aqueducts, bridges, and tunnels. Amazingly, even after more than 2,000 years many Roman structures remain.

A significant boost to understanding the necessity of language and the social cooperation needed for continued advancement of civilization was documentation of the steady progress in the legal, technological, and cultural systems. That meant documenting historic events and newfound knowledge in a format called a "book." Precisely tracing the development of language from its inception is considered ancient Sumerian around 2,100 BC in the city-state of Uruk. It was a mythological narrative about an actual ruler of Uruk. Estimates have been made by historians that this feat was accomplished 1,500 years before Genesis was written. The book, "The Epic of Gilgamesh," was originally written on clay tablets and amazingly a clay tablet copy has survived 4,100 years and remains in the British Museum.

Language and books have been instrumental in civilization's march towards advancing Western Culture by recording humanity's unpredictable but successful achievements. The quality of history's record keeping steadily improved with the advent of language and preserving information in books.

Many years after the first book was written, there was a great invention that amazingly served the world for the better by preserving and spreading knowledge. Johannes Gutenberg, a goldsmith, initiated the "printing revolution" in 1440 when he developed the first movable-type printing press. This technology improved rapidly and soon spread throughout Europe, assisting all fields of endeavors from religion to history and science.

The Enlightenment and the steady growth of Christian influence throughout the world flourished with this revolution in mass communication that changed the world and provided a great boost to civilization.

The printing press arrived in Colonial America in the mid-17th century, motivated by the demand for more religious literature and in time for Ben Franklin, Thomas Paine, William Bradford, and others to do a little "pamphleteering" in support of the American Revolutionary War. Circulation was not over-regulated at that time and news spread swiftly, providing tremendous benefit to those planning and carrying out the revolution against British tyranny and especially emphasizing its relationship to the principle of liberty.

Four hundred years after Gutenberg's inventing the printing press, Western Civilization got a gigantic shot in the arm with Samuel Morse's development of the electric telegraph, which ushered in the modern age of communications. Previous inventions dealing with electricity by Alessandro Volta and Hans Christian Oersted enhanced the successful efforts of Morse to send that first and famous message by telegraph on May 24, in 1844 from D.C. to Baltimore: "What has God Wrought?"

Travel time across the Atlantic has continued to shrink. In 1492, on wind power, it took Columbus, two months to make the trip. With the help of technology's steady improvements, the first non-stop airplane flight in 1927 made it in 34 hours. And in 1996 the Concorde cut that down to 2 hours and 52 minutes.

All the previous discoveries that led to these historical events and the many others that would soon follow, were soon to be recognized as contributions to the ongoing Industrial Revolution. The telegraph had an immediate and profound effect on world-wide communications in all fields of endeavor, from finance to warfare to the dissemination of news, while keeping up with the influence of the various religions. Information, the lifeblood of civilization, now circles the globe at the speed of light.

Impressively, in 1866, a mere twenty years after the telegraph was first tested in 1844, a permanent telegraph cable was laid between the United States and Europe. The enthusiasm for this development led the way to a modern age of communications with the subsequent inventions of the telephone, the facsimile machine, radio, television, the internet, and block chain technology.

But another huge advancement was yet to come. In 1947 the US developed the first silicon transistor. This new development was soon recognized as a magnificent technological breakthrough, and early on it was difficult to fully comprehend the full significance of the practical use of semiconductors.

A big question remains: Has the concept and availability of liberty to the world kept pace with the advancement of technology? The contest between science and the higher law is similar to that between technology for peace and prosperity or war.

We are now witnessing an explosion of new information and the discovery of the mysteries and deeply-held secrets of endless space which are unlimited for human comprehension while prompting spiritual contemplation of the vastness and unmeasurable expansion of the universe. Steadily, over the centuries, the estimated size of the universe and the number of stars and galaxies that exists has become incomprehensible.

To me it seems a bit strange that most of the scientists who sense the ever-growing size and immensity of the universe never bump into the Creator in their observations. Personally, I find many scientists have a greater "faith" than I do: "faith" that the true magnificence of the universe can all be explained by "potluck," quantum physics, and the principle of gravity. The "God of Creation" might be more likely found by looking inward rather than scanning the estimated 400 billion stars in the Milky Way alone. Not to mention the estimated billions of other galaxies whose numbers continue to rapidly expand.

Spirituality and science were active participants used by the Founders in the development of Western Civilization and culture, and if Western Civilization is to survive, we'll need to continue using them.

But the industrial-technological revolution of the past three centuries was much more than the telegraph, space travel, semiconductors, and block chain technology. The progress achieved during this entire period identified the concept of "Western Civilization" as the most advanced culture in recorded history. The many discoveries and cultural advancements in this 300-year period have easily outclassed and outperformed the recognized significance of human progress of the 5000 years prior to the arrival of Western Civilization.

Many varied events stood out as being especially beneficial to human progress. In a response to food shortages, the mistakes of protectionism and war had put England in dire straits. The repeal of the "corn laws" in 1846 by the British, led by John Bright and Richard Cobden, initiated an age of free trade and the obvious benefits it provided made obvious the need to reject the many shortcomings of protectionism. This has been of great significance in striving for peace and prosperity by expanding personal liberty. Free trade today is under attack, needlessly undermining a valuable policy for promoting prosperity.

Getting rid of the long-time tradition that the "king" owned the patents for all new inventions inspired a surge in development of additional manual labor-saving tools and machinery. Any hint of the government increasing the liberty of the people, including the right of intellectual property ownership, protected by contract, greatly inspired the creative activities that served the wellbeing of everyone.

More recently, abandoning the flawed concept of "the labor theory of value," which was shared by Adam Smith and Karl Marx, provided a thorough awareness on how real "value" is calculated, giving a boost to understanding how a free-market economy works.

America's contribution to modern civilization

The spirit of America that inspired the Colonists to declare independence in 1776 from the authoritarian British Empire set the stage for the passage of the Constitution in 1787.These two events provided a tremendous boost for advancing Western Civilization, culturally and economically. The Constitution, although flawed, was soon recognized as the best effort ever made to promote the cause of personal liberty by reining in abusive government power.

To achieve this, they had to bring together the "Founders-to-be" of America. This was a unique group of well-educated individuals, knowledgeable, spiritual, and aware of what was at stake in continuing civilization's steady progress. The odds were against them; the dangers were self-evident.

The spiritual beliefs that the Founders generally shared, were a strong belief in a God of Creation and a discernment of a higher law. They shared the belief that anyone who so chose could easily distinguish between good and evil and reject nihilism whenever it showed its ugly presence. They recognized that the higher law was the most powerful force to repel the evil doers' constant effort to gain political power. American revolutionaries eagerly joined in the conflict that they readily understood and were already engaged in. They knew they were living in the middle of a very special historic period, of great significance referred to as the "Enlightenment".

The motivation that drove the designers of the American Republic was a shared spiritual belief in "Divine Providence," with a strong distaste for the authoritarian danger of pure democracy. Over the centuries, pure democracy had been used to justify contrived majorities to serve as the final arbiter of fairness and equity. It was the Founders' opinion that individual rights would not be protected by the dictates of a manufactured authoritarian majority. Rights, instead, were understood to be inalienable, coming from God; not from a government appointed by an ill-defined majority and ripe for corruption. The problems we face today result from the accumulated power of the lobbyists and the special interests, who through a corrupt legal system have been able to bamboozle the "majority" into believing that the liberty they claimed to cherish will be protected. Eventually, however, it will be discovered that both liberty and its fake prosperity have been sacrificed on the altar of the false god of democracy. America should have paid more attention to Thomas Jefferson than Alexander Hamilton in this regard.

A dictatorship of the majority is more malleable and liberty is more at risk in a democracy than in a republic. With a casual look at the mess we're in today, it's easy to see why the enemies of liberty are solidly behind the cult's preaching the gospel of majoritarianism, something they can freely manipulate, while the principles that inspired the Declaration of Independence are maligned and subject to modern day censorship by the combined forces of corporatism and an overzealous government. None of the Founders wanted a democracy. They understood how dangerous majorities were to liberty and they were in no mood to risk their lives for it. Their resistance reflected the knowledge they had gained through the study of history and philosophy, while witnessing the ongoing progress associated with the Enlightenment, and their conviction that "divine providence" was on their side.

The nature of the Founders' education

The Founders were not handicapped by a government "department of education." Their education was crucial to their ability to make the moral and political case for revolution against the most powerful nation of their time. In their desire to present the case for the liberty, they justly argued it belonged to all individuals as a natural right and were quite aware of the grave danger that lie ahead in pursuing this cause.

Most historians have agreed that the Founding Fathers, regardless of age or background, received a full-fledged exposure to "classical education." It was commonly understood that "wisdom and virtue" were to be the guiding precepts in their goal of establishing a unique form of government, designed to protect the liberty of the people and not the wealth and power of the few privileged elite. They were well aware of other unsuccessful previous attempts to achieve this in theory. This time, the Founders were optimistic, believing that Providence would guide their newest attempt to established a political system dedicated to the cause of liberty.

Martin Cothren, in his article "The Classical Education of the Founding Fathers," thoroughly described what education was like in the 18th Century. As an example, to be admitted to King's College (Columbia University) required "mastery of Greek and Latin grammar, reading three orations from Cicero and Vergil's Aeneid in the original Latin and translating the first ten chapters of the Gospel of John from Greek into Latin." Cothran explained that liberal arts were strongly emphasized, which included: grammar, logic, rhetoric, arithmetic, geometry, astronomy, and music.

In Contrast, out of the hundreds of members of Congress I met over the years, there were probably only a half dozen who were aware of one of the greatest economists of the 20th Century, Ludwig Von Mises. America's educational system leaves a lot to be desired since the current system is in a free fall, chopping away at a civilization that took centuries to build.

America's contributions to building Western Civilization and its subsequent pernicious undermining of it

Thomas Jefferson deservedly received major credit for formulating the principles of America's plan to establish a "new" Republic. Much of the philosophic substance of the Declaration of Independence is easily traceable to John Locke, whose views significantly influenced Jefferson's political philosophy. The age of the Enlightenment, during which these two champions for liberty lived, provided a fertile field to plant the seeds of the American Revolution. This played an important role in the 19th and 20th Century's contributions to furthering the developments of "Western Civilization." A favorite Jefferson quote that challenged the nihilism that pervades most political systems and instead supports the higher law concept of morality is direct to this point: "Honesty is the first chapter in the book of wisdom." This seems to have been completely forgotten in current times.

There were several well-debated issues at that time, shared by Locke and Jefferson, that found their way into the Declaration of Independence and the Constitution. Both agreed on the principle of "natural rights" and some form of social compact that included equal justice for all and that government authority should be based on the consent of the people.

Within this concept, it was recognized that there was an obvious moral prohibition against harming others or stealing their property. According to Locke and Jefferson, protecting life, liberty, and property was best achieved by strictly limiting the size and scope of government. These views were generally endorsed by all the Founders or the Revolution would not have occurred. Locke was also emphatic that "sovereignty resides in the people" and that authoritarianism should be consistently rejected. One amazing tidbit relating to the writing of the Declaration of Independence, was that Jefferson was all of 33 years old in 1776!

The principle of the 'separation of church and state'

This Principle of religious freedom was a major issue discussed at the time of America's founding and served as the motivation for drafting and amending the Constitution with a "Bill of Rights." This issue had motivated a large number of European and British immigrants to colonize America in the 17th Century. The Founders, who insisted on a more explicit protection of personal liberty, were determined to make it crystal clear that religious freedom was a paramount concern for them. Though the Constitution was written in 1787, ratified in 1788, and commenced operation in 1789, the dispute over how to guarantee the specific right of religious freedom had not been resolved. It took another three years for the Bill of Rights to be added to the original Constitution in 1791. It represented a victory for the Anti-Federalists over the Federalists who saw this addition as a challenge to their desire for a strong centralized government. This popular demand for the protection of Separation of Church and State led to a generalized concern for maximizing the protection of all personal rights which led to the much more expanded "Bill of Rights."

James Madison was credited for drafting the document, but the inspiration came from Jefferson whose argument for the passage of the Bill of Rights included this statement: "A Bill of Rights is what the people are entitled to against every government on earth, general or particular, and what no just government should refuse" (Jefferson: December 20, 1787).

Locke consistently opposed authoritarianism as a proper policy for governance if the moral principle of "natural rights" is to be respected. Locke had strongly argued in his "Letter Concerning Toleration," for Separation of Church and State; a position eagerly accepted by Jefferson. This position was defended by the use of "reason in seeking truth for the benefit of the individual and society, in both material and spiritual matters," while recognizing it as part of "the divine purpose for Humanity." This belief was frequently referred to by the Founders as "Divine Providence," believing it guided them in the risky effort to establish a special type of Republic and pursue the independence of the colonies from the British Empire.

The importance of this burning issue of guaranteeing religious freedom led to that issue becoming the First Amendment to the Constitution. Its declaration sent a very clear message, mincing no words in its FIRST phrase: "Congress shall make no law respecting an establishment of religion or prohibiting the free exercise thereof," and to fortify this liberty, it would be further protected by the protection of freedom of speech, the press, assembly, and the right to petition the government.

To date, the principle of Separation of Church and State has been generally endorsed and followed by our government. However, Americans are now becoming leery about our government's encroachment of religious freedom, along with concern for all the other protected First Amendment's rights. We witnessed a calloused disregard for personal liberty during the unconstitutional lockdowns during the Covid hysteria when even church attendance was being curtailed. This should be a wake-up call for all of us.

Genghis Khan: Jefferson's ally for religious freedom

In considering Genghis Khan's political beliefs and reputation, it seemed that he couldn't possibly have been a candidate for favorably influencing Thomas Jefferson in his efforts to enshrine the principle of religious freedom into the recently passed American Constitution in 1787. Khan's reputation over the centuries has been that of a "ruthless tyrant" who built the largest ever contiguous land empire.

Khan founded the Mongol Empire in 1206 AD which lasted until 1368 AD when it was dissolved

But thanks to New York Times bestselling author Jack Weatherford in his book, "Genghis Khan and the Quest for God" (2016), a fascinating "foot-note" to history was revealed regarding Khan's influence on Jefferson's final version of the First Amendment designed to protect religious liberty. Khan was born in 1162 AD and died in 1227 AD. Five hundred and eighty-five years after the founding of the Mongolian Empire in 1206 AD, America's Bill of Rights, in 1791, was added to the recently passed Constitution. Good ideas have a life of their own and obviously are long-lasting.

Although Khan was an authoritarian leader who used violence to build history's largest land-mass empire, whose victims numbered in the millions, one is prompted to inquire about his economic and political views. His achievements, as head of the empire, were not related only to his military prowess. His "Code of Laws," relating to his economic and social policies, were significant as well.

The "Code" was identified as the "Yassa" which followed Khan's personal desires, combined with various tribal customs. His "First Law" was revealing: "It is ordered to believe that there is only one God, creator of heaven and earth, who alone gives life and death, riches and poverty as pleases Him and who has over everything an absolute power." The "Code's" Third Law dealt with electing an emperor: A new emperor "shall be proclaimed" when "he has been elected previously by princes, Khans, officers, and other Mongol nobles in a general council." It sounds to me like an Electoral College! Other laws provided severe punishments for theft, spying for the enemy, lying, or being a false witness.

Genghis's development of Uyghur script helped to unify his massive empire while enhancing his political control. Other important policies he supported were meritocracy, lower taxes, development of cohesiveness of the great Silk Road, and support for "free trade," which included trade with essentially all of Asia and most importantly Christian Europe. These policies promoted historic cultural and economic benefits to the empire and like the principle of religious freedom that Genghis strongly promoted, have had a long-lasting world-wide effect, even contributing to the development of Western Civilization.

Religious freedom according to Genghis Khan

Genghis Khan became one of the world's greatest promoters of religious freedom. He set up an Institution responsible for the protection of complete religious liberty for all the citizens, plus tax exemption for government, military, and social service participants as well for all religious leaders, including physicians.

Weatherford, in his detailed and historically significant discussion of Khan's strong defense of religious freedom and how it came to influence Thomas Jefferson's wording of the First Amendment, is fascinating reading.

In his research he discovered that the most popular book in America, in the 18th Century was, "The History of Genghizcan the Great," published by a French scholar in 1710. It was an "authoritative and lengthy biography" of the great Khan. Benjamin Franklin sold many copies of the book in the colonies, by mail order, from the Philadelphia post office. Weatherford's thorough research of these mailing records revealed which of the Founding Fathers had an interest in the views of a dictator who reigned five hundred years before.

Weatherford diligently sought for evidence that there was a direct connection to John Locke who was recognized to have influenced Jefferson on the importance of religious freedom and other freedom issues. None were found. But he continued to search for any information that supported a more direct interest by the Founders in "Genghis Khan's Great Law." It was Martha Washington's gift of a book to her husband that sparked some interest in this wild search for evidence that Genghis Khan did influence an event that contributed to the Constitution's clarity on religious liberty and Western Civilization. The book that Martha gave to her husband was "a novelized biography of Genghis Khan, published in French in 1691," and translated into English the following year. Although, after three hundred years, the book can still be found in the library at Mount Vernon, there's no evidence that anybody ever read it, making it hard to use it as strong evidence that it had influenced George Washington on the subject of religious freedom.

That was a disappointment to Weatherford, but he continued in his pursuit for concrete evidence that Genghis had an influence on the final version of the First Amendment to the US Constitution. He soon came across new evidence that showed multiple book sales of the most popular book on Genghis Khan; "The history of Genghizcan the Great, First Emperor of The Mongols and Tartars" which was purchased by many colonists. The book was promoted by Ben Franklin in his newspaper contributing to the many copies that were sold throughout the colonies. No evidence could be found to show that Franklin had a special interest in the subject of religious freedom.

Weatherford's detailed search for some objective evidence that the Founders might have been influenced by Genghis Khan finally came to fruition. He discovered that the Founder who purchased the most copies the Genghis Khan's biography was Thomas Jefferson, one of which ended up in the US Library of Congress and another in the Library of the University of Virginia. It's assumed that many of his colleagues received copies from him.

The main issue that guided Jefferson in finalizing his understanding was looking for the most practical way to put the principle of religious freedom into law. What Jefferson found was: "religious freedom was an individual right. not a prerogative of the church." It sounds like the point then became that religious freedom did not require a church or synagogue etc. to enjoy the benefits of religious liberty. Jefferson makes the final point in the First Amendment: "No laws prohibiting the establishment of religion or freely expressing one's spiritual views."

It thus can be argued that Genghis Khan's strong belief in religious freedom, economic policies that made sense, and his success in unifying a huge empire with views, were actually positive for developing Western Civilization. He demonstrated that a huge empire made up of many religious factions that were constantly at war with each other, along with many tribes and various social customs, could live together more harmoniously when influenced by Genghis's views on religious freedom and adapting to the principle of meritocracy in trade and general economic policy.

We in the United States, have drifted a long way from a social-economic system based on merit, and instead have replaced it with a steady move towards the cult of "Wokeism." and socialist type economic equality. This has provoked a destructive "war" between those who accept nihilism's rejection of truth and the "remnant" that clings to the belief in a higher law.

Maybe a better current understanding of the philosophic views of Genghis Khan could help us preserve the many achievements provided to us by Western Civilization. Is it possible that we're in the process of accepting a social-economic system less thoughtful than Khan's primitive Empire? If that is so, that means we should expect that a more primitive Western Civilization lies ahead. Many thoughtful people are already of that opinion. Knowing just who stole Western Civilization is required if this trend is to be reversed. It's worth a try.

Who's responsible for Western Civilization's decline?

Civilization as we know it today had its origination many centuries ago. Estimates are that the Sumerian civilization began three to four thousand years, BC. It is estimated that the Sumerian language produced the first linguistic record of Sumerian more than 3000 years ago. It could be argued that this was one of the first step for establishing a process for steadily accumulating and passing on knowledge that facilitated the advancement of the human race, reaching tremendous heights in the current period, now referred to as Western Civilization. This effort allowed for continuous preserving and improving cultural, scientific, and intellectual matters relating to art, literature, music, medicine, economics, and philosophic ideas. To say the least, a lot has been accomplished and recorded since the Sumerians initiated the process of building on past discoveries, and now have reached the heights of the past century with many amazing advancements having been accomplished in the past 250 years.

We now are witnessing a challenge to the inexorable successes in the development and improvements of Western Civilization that have occurred over thousands of years. Are we destined to systematically destroy our current civilization in a much shorter period of time than it took to build it?

Since this threat is real, it's prompting many people to ask: Who's responsible for this coming event? Over the six thousand years since the first book was written, mankind, despite many obstacles, engaged in activity that produced a society that benefitted from once unimaginable technical inventions that enhanced the comforts of the human race. Pragmatic needs, reason, and science, all played a part in promoting the advancement of civilization. At times this progress was challenged by the negative effects of constant wars that fostered the redistribution of wealth from the conquered to the conquerors. Some have wrongly argued that war can be justified as an economic benefit to the people forced into participating in it. But almost always liberty is lost in war. The only exception is if the war or revolution is authentic in that it is being fought to protect or gain the natural right to life and liberty from morally depraved authoritarians. Over these many years of building Western Civilization, compensating for a poor understanding of economic law has been necessary.

It has been argued that Western Civilization peaked during the Enlightenment of the eighteenth century, at a time when celebrating the Age of Reason was commonplace. Certainly, America's Declaration of Independence and the writing of the Constitution was inspired by the spirit of liberty that existed at that particular time. It was a time when reason became an ally of both liberty and religion, with science making great strides in advancing modern civilization despite man's shortcomings.

Early on we were warned by the American Founders about the fragile nature of our Constitution. Many now fear that much of Western Civilization is under threat. John Adams was precise in his admonition that more was required than a well-written Constitution to maintain a true republic that promoted peace and prosperity: "Our Constitution was made only for a moral and religious people. It is wholly inadequate to the government of any other." Today, the moral bankruptcy of America is readily apparent and is recognized as a significant factor in our effort to identify those who were responsible for joining the "Coup that stole Western Civilization."

Though imperfect and man-created, through thousands of years of steady progress that built the unique Western Civilization mankind has generally accepted the notion that only with the "protection of divine Providence" was the climatic result — the establishment of American Republic — made possible.

Today, nihilism's influence has erased the once more-commonly held belief, that a "higher law" prevailed and that spirituality, Christianity, non-violence, and property ownership were respected and could not be "canceled" by a government controlled "speech police"

Just as the building of Western Civilization engaged many diverse groups, the enemies of civilization have now banded together, driven by hate and avarice, seeking ill-gotten power to be used to destroy the benefits of living in a civilized world. For some in this group even war has become a proper tool for population control.

The sad part of all of this is that truth is always sacrificed in an age of nihilism. Logic, likewise, is dismissed as not being beneficial in the lawless society that it has created. Lies are deified and truth is vilified. The chaos that is created satisfies the nihilists in their effort to first destroy civilization based on the higher law, which they hate, and then create a new social order where authoritarianism assumes political control...for the good of the people, of course!

Philosophically, the Enlightenment and the birth of the American Republic reflected a special time in human history amidst the giant strides made in advancing civilization. The momentum of these improvements continued into the Twentieth Century, but now we're witnessing a systemic erosion of the moral values of the people and our political leaders who are required by the Constitution to maintain a republic within Western Civilization.

The 'Surreptitious Coup'

The Coup's goal was to replace our current political and economic system, which was built on knowledge accumulated over many centuries and inspired by the principles of personal liberty and natural law as guides for advancing civilization.

The surreptitious Coup to dismantle Western Civilization has been ongoing for many decades. This is something new and more significant than the many disruptions in the history of the growing influence of Western Civilization that were overcome by renewed enthusiasm for advancing cultural and scientific developments over the past several hundred years. This current challenge, though widespread in the Western world, is being especially directed toward America, the unchallenged leader of Western Civilization since WWII.

The goal of this sinister and somewhat invisible coup is to destroy the miracles generated by the enthusiasm of the Enlightenment since the late 17th Century, along with America's contribution to the spirit of liberty and including an energized market economy. The bitter enemies of civilized society that we face today are ignoramuses, driven by the defeatism of nihilism, with a full-throated rejection of the "higher law," that has smothered them with a sense of insecurity. Without any understanding or interest in the natural law, the perpetrators are incapable of experiencing guilt or shame, which to them is a mysterious concept. Sociopaths are that way. To help explain the dilemma, one must realize that the participants are the "philosophic" descendants of the Barbarians who finally brought the Roman Empire to an end after it was weakened from within.

We now face a similar situation as the perpetrators of the ongoing "Coup" celebrate the disintegration of Western culture, loss of economic prosperity, rejection of traditional morality and family values, tolerance of government corruption, militarism that generates constant wars, and a lawless judicial system that provides "legal protection" to the political party that is most dedicated to the ring leaders of the Coup. Hollywood has been placed in charge of all "Sunday Schools" and government kindergartens as it participates in convincing leaders of the Coup that the "village," even when just pretending to promote spirituality, is more qualified for raising a child to accept obedience to the state than parents. The naïve expectations of the government "village," with promises of nirvana, permitted their false promises to destroy our once great cities. Instead, we ended up with the victims enduring the squalor and poverty of homelessness and their streets turned into open sewers; all deliberately created by foolish government policies and evil motives.

The enemy who robbed

The theft of Western Civilization and the tragic disintegration of the promises of the American Republic cannot be ignored. Our survival depends on it. The "Coup" must be exposed. It cannot remain "Surreptitious." The Coup appears victorious as it's nearly complete with a continuous push for more barbarism and violent chaos. Those who reject the principle of truth in their effort to establish a dictatorial society are pleased with the result.

As bad as it is, there is no reason to believe that reversing the trend is impossible. But this can't be accomplished without an understanding of the basic principles required to maintain a civilized society. There's no reason why we must surrender to uncivilized barbarism. It's not meant to be.

A major problem though, is that authoritarianism has smashed the principles of non-aggression and voluntarism that had been carved out of a favorable political environment created by the Enlightenment and the birth of the American Republic in the 18th Century. This had proved to be highly beneficial to Western Civilization. But destroying America's grand experiment of a libertarian society also threatens the wonders acquired in the development of Western Civilization.

What would the Founders think of the conditions we have burdened ourselves with if they were to return today to see how things were going? My guess is they would be more disappointed than surprised. They might also remind us of their warnings of what is required for a constitution to protect the people's liberty from the evildoers who mocked anyone showing reverence for the "higher law."

John Adams succinctly identified the threat that the newly created American Republic faced: the "Constitution was made only for a moral and religious people. It is wholly inadequate to the government of any other." The Founders, I am sure, would not be bragging today about the character of the politicians and the members of the special interest groups who are in charge in Washington.

Many loopholes still exist that provide a fertile field for those who diligently work to scrape what is left from the "rule of law," while the fools willingly acquiesce to the power that the victors of the "Coup" now control.

Beware of those conditions that facilitate the continuous effort to "cancel" any activity, philosophic or actual, that cling to or promote the benefits of Western Civilization including our Constitutional Republic. Every effort should be made to identify the persons or groups responsible for the radical destruction of our civilization and, while doing so, gain wealth and power.

Handmaidens of the Coup

A host of conditions has facilitated the Coup's effort to destroy Western Civilization and bring about a very much negatively-changed America.

The admitted goal of Cultural Marxism is to produce as much societal chaos as possible in preparing to rebuild a "new and better" authoritarian "paradise:"

Moral standards reflect nihilist beliefs that truth is not knowable.

Economic theories taught in our universities for more than a hundred years are deeply flawed and have created a dangerous political system of wealth mal-distribution.

Most universities side with the beliefs of the "Woke" cult on social and philosophic issues by punishing honest debate and permitting the use of violence to "cancel" it. Conservative Republicans and libertarians are considered pariahs and are being discriminated against by most universities "banning" them from campuses.

Fortunately, despite the FBI and other government

agencies' incestuous relationships with social media, the internet, and other forms of communication, we can still support a determined remnant to pursue the truth in all matters: philosophic, social, political, scientific, economic, and spiritual.

The nihilist enemies of liberty can suppress, ignore, ridicule, and even kill people who defend truth, but they cannot kill truth. Eventually their attacks amplify the truth. It's been tried many times before and always fails. The remnant always prevails.

It's been reported that the control of free speech by the Wokeism cult, has succeeded in intimidating 60 percent of college students into refraining from expressing their views. Students have been known to be blacklisted by merely mentioning words like "Southern Heritage" or "Dixie." This is indoctrination, which is the opposite of education.

The fake debate over the First Amendment is a distraction from the dangerous collusion between the media, especially the social media, and various government agencies that are capable of rigging the news, stealing elections, and terrorizing the people with gross distortions of epidemics that serve the financial interests of pharmaceutical corporations. The use of the FBI to punish or reward government-approved speech is a disgrace. Let's hope that America soon wakes up and boldly reclaims the fundamental and basic natural right of free expression. Without it, liberty perishes. First Amendment arguments can be easily resolved with a clear understanding of private property ownership, voluntary contracts, and the prohibition on slander and libel. In order to attain real freedom of speech, the FBI would need to be abolished.

The destructiveness of the Covid lockdown has significantly accelerated the deterioration of all government-controlled education and medical care.

Politicians' promises of "free stuff" have created the largest debt the world has ever witnessed, but it will be liquidated one way or another. The only choice is whether it will be by "inflation" or "deflation."

The true private property concept has been abandoned and replaced with a deeply flawed system of "corporatism" and collective ownership of all property.

The credibility of our government continues to decline, and deservedly so. Investigations, commissions, election rhetoric, and especially the oath of office each member takes, are not believable to a very large number of Americans. Ironically this includes those who benefit (short term) from the goods stolen from the tax slaves who have to pay the bills. It should surprise no one that the people are getting poorer and angrier and forced to pay for policies that always fail.

Elections are now routinely challenged as a consequence of the phony "Russiagate" scandal. This phenomenon will turn out to be much more serious than has yet been realized. Old fashioned politics is part of it, but unrestrained hatred and jealousy toward Donald Trump will be recognized as having incited tremendous immoral and illegal activity. The big question is whether the collusion of the FBI and the social media participants will ever be brought to justice or even get a slap on the wrist?

The Coup has devastated the socio-economic system

of most of the West by supporting the radicalism of many destructive policies like Antifa, Black Lives Matter, government takeover of the private practice of medicine, transgenderism, and attacks on "traditional and Christian values." With the banning of all pronouns, everyone has become an "it."

Marriage is defined by a totally intolerant government, when instead it should be the participants' prerogative to define their own marriage, without government interference in legislating spiritual matters.

Radical proponents of abortion justify eliminating the life of a human fetus with an unrelated bizarre assertion that the rejection of abortion takes away "reproductive rights." This is nonsense easily refuted by Biology 101.

With the steady erosion of the resistance against tyranny by the people, the Coup operatives have responded by taking advantage of the social chaos that they created. This satisfies their desires to build a utopian socialist state by destroying much of what had been achieved during the 20th Century.

A pure fiat monetary system generates unlimited special interest groups seeking funds for warfare and welfare at the expense of honest work and self-reliance. Every effort throughout history that claimed to make a fiat system long-lasting and beneficial to the masses has failed miserably. Because the fiat money system is based on fraud and government force, the ultimate outcome becomes known a long time before the recipients are willing to admit to themselves that it was all a scam AND that a price must be paid for their delusional hopes of an easy road to riches.

DEBT is a ruthless ruler

The degree of danger can be measured by the size of the debt, the extent of malinvestments, the absence of real savings, the erosion of personal liberty, and the social upheaval among the special interests fighting over the crumbs the super-rich throw to the poor. The chaos, which is deliberately designed by the Cultural Marxists, permits the Coup to expand its dictatorial powers and move toward a total victory for the "unenlightened," while the FRIENDS of the "Enlightenment" are sent to the "critical care unit," with Dr. Fauci in charge, for resuscitation. The $31 trillion debt is pervasive. It was concocted in a manner similar to the deliberate chaos that was created in our social-economic system.

What the conspirators don't realize is that the size of the debt and the severity of the moral crisis will not allow many Americans to escape paying their share of the bill that is required to liquidate the debt. Few realize that there's no chance whatsoever that the liquidation can be avoided. In the process, much wealth will be destroyed and what's left will fall into the hands of those who are capable and willing to use force to seize it. It's already happening. An effort must be made to find individuals willing to support the option that can nullify the pain and suffering that the Marxist policies cause and replace it with policies that are based on voluntarism and liberty.

This requires the rejection of authoritarianism and its use of aggressive force for bringing about political changes.

The Coup by stealth stole Western Civilization and gave us the age of deceit

Western Civilization was developed over many centuries by bits and pieces, but by the 17th Century it was ready for an explosion of unbelievable advancement in human endeavors. This was achieved in spite of the inability to stop the almost constant wars that have engulfed the world. Those who benefitted from the profits of war and the political power they provided were rarely concerned about advancing Western Civilization. Despite the challenge from the warmongers' destructive nature, those who sought to use the technological development of the past 300 years for peaceful purposes continued the progress of civilization into the 20th Century.

The Enlightenment was estimated to have started around 1685 and ended in 1815 when it gave way to Romanticism in the early 19th Century. Romanticism was a countermovement to the Enlightenment that arose from criticisms over the former's excessive emphasis on science and reason. Romanticism's influence lasted for about 50 years and was a response to the clamor that ushered in the age of those seeking an emphasis on "realism."

The Age of Realism started around 1850 and lasted well into the 20th Century, a period of time in which it became clear to even the casual observer that something very significant was happening to Western Civilization and the American Republic. Some of the greatest achievements of all time had been packed into the notion of modern civilization, and in spite of the apparent benefits we still enjoy, legitimate concerns regarding the future have arisen.

Confidence regarding peace, prosperity, and even survival has been greatly diminished.

The 20th century is destined to become known as a century when Western Civilization came unraveled and America's grand experiment with personal liberty was stolen by a surreptitious Coup. The recognition of this tragic act is becoming more apparent every day.

How did this come about? A moral, financial, and philosophic bankruptcy in a complicit nation, blinded by delusions of an idyllic society, driven by power-hungry politicians, brainwashed by progressive universities, explains it. Bad ideas have bad consequences. Allow evil authoritarians to gain political power and social influence and this is what you get: the greatest political Coup in history.

No one should be surprised. If this usurpation of power is not dealt with, the deterioration of the "West," and especially America, will continue to accelerate as it rapidly moves toward tyranny. However, those who benefit from the Coup by gaining wealth and political power will not be able to contain the tragic results that have been dumped on the compliant masses. We should expect that violence will result in the counter-revolution against the insanities pushed on normal people by the nihilists who canceled "truth" and forced upon us an "Age of Deceit" that made lying morally acceptable, popular, and profitable under the pretense of humanitarianism and equity.

The lying mentality "justifies" the profound ritual of the politicians reciting their oaths of office without a second thought. "Petty" lies regarding a politician's bio can be used endlessly by the opposition, but for truly criminal activities it all depends on the whim of the Deep State's use of social media and which party is in charge of the FBI and CIA.

Sadly, the bigger the lie, the more likely it will receive strong bipartisan support. The people will be conditioned to accept the lies as their patriotic duty, no matter how horrible the consequences will be. These lies are the ones designed to protect or expand "The Empire." The hopes and desires of the authors of the Constitution, in their desire to limit unauthorized war, never materialized. A president, by executive order, can start a war without Congressional approval lasting decades and "justified" by grotesque lies that caused the death of millions of people. One report claimed that the US has been involved in a war 225 out of the 243 years since the Declaration of Independence with only five officially declared.

Domestically, the Covid war against civil liberties virtually destroyed the First Amendment and severely undermined the private practice of medicine. The CDC and the pharmaceutical industry's takeover were mostly done by Executive Orders while totally ignoring the Constitution. Telling the truth during the fake pandemic caused the truth-tellers to be banned and even lose their jobs.

Good v. Evil: Mankind's 5,000 years search and still looking

Over the centuries, many individuals from different political and ethnic groups claimed they had special insight into knowing the difference between right and wrong. All early legal codes dealt with the issue of deciding the proper — many times harsh — penalties for those who disobeyed the law handed down by the various governments. These laws were profuse and complex but interestingly on certain issues they followed a similar pattern.

The best known "code" that influenced Western Civilization was the Ten Commandments. The Commandments dealt with individual rights and property, including rules regarding personal moral behavior. The admonition against killing, cheating, stealing, lying, and coveting are all very libertarian principles emphasizing truth and rejection of aggression. Property ownership was assumed to be proper and contracts were to be followed.

It is estimated that the Ten Commandments were written in about the 7th century BC or nearly 3,000 years ago. The principle of a higher law was clearly recognizable in this document.

The Code of Hammurabi was written approximately 700 years prior to the Ten Commandments and it too had legal similarities: recognizing property right and integrity of contract while establishing punishment for lying, cheating, stealing, or causing the death of another person.

Even prior to the Hammurabi Code, around 4,000 years ago, the first known written legal code was inscribed on clay tablets in Sumer, Mesopotamia. All three codes, dating back to 2100 BC revealed a belief in a higher authority that guided moral behavior and imposed punishment for those who disobeyed.

Yet today, as we witness the attacks on Western Civilization, we see a correlation between the rejection of the fundamental principle of truth that distinguishes right from wrong, and the ability of people to live harmoniously with each other. If this message, known to mankind from the beginning of recorded history, is ignored we will see the further erosion of civilization's progress that brought the human race out of the stone age and primitive living conditions. "Canceling" the effort for seeking TRUTH, as some currently propose, cancels man's spiritual nature and the material benefits that flow from civilization.

The birth of the grand Coup

America's Progressive era ushered in the 20th Century with a gross distortion of the meaning of the word "progressive." Selling the idea of progressivism to the American people as something positive is a joke and a lie. It instead should have been referred to as a "regressive" move: It has turned out to be a long-term plan to challenge the notion of a "higher law" and usher in an era of nihilism. This takeover was accomplished by a very successful Coup and was done surreptitiously. No army invaded us, and the politicians' false promises were welcomed and believed. Living off previously created wealth and paying for it with perpetually rising debt guaranteed complacency by the recipients of these "free" benefits. The Coup's ongoing expansion and influence spread its political power over worldwide financial and social institutions.

The crisis we face today is not a result of natural causes. It is a result of the Coup's ongoing success in remaking the world based on lies and evil goals.

We now find the benefits of Western Civilization under siege as a result. Concluding that the destructive changes of the last 120 years are a result of progressivism's influence is the only way we will have a chance to reverse this trend.

In the early years of this effort, their goals were easily identified: A contrived war with Spain; passage of the income tax; establishment of the IRS; creation of the Federal Reserve monster. Woodrow Wilson's foreign policy of "making the world safe for democracy" pushed the US foolishly into WWI. This set the stage for FDR's conniving for our participation in these foolish policies like getting into WWII, thus providing supporters a chance to falsely claim the nonsense that it ended the Great Depression.

These events were driven by the Coup conspirators with their long-term plans to undermine the American Republic and cast aside Western Civilization's advancements in order to promote a society that rejects the higher laws of liberty and replaces them with a Marxist type of collectivism.

They soon recognized that their ultimate goals had to be kept a deeply held secret. Systematically though, these plans did serve the interests of the Coup's long-term effort to destroy the Republic and substitute it with Marxist-type system.

The individuals and various groups that have supported the Coup are amorphous in nature, but the greatest motivation for most of them has included many personal reasons. Their enthusiasm came from those who disliked or even hated the defenders of Western Civilization for their moral and spiritual values that were used to justify civilization's existence and benefits. Seeking truth has never been on the agenda of those who have seductively whittled away at our Republic and the principles of liberty.

"Wokeism" has attracted millions of supporters under the false pretense of equity, fairness, and saving "planet Earth," while denying its destructive nature. Political pressure and alliances within social media systematically organized anti-science propaganda, government driven medical mandates, and the "epidemic" growth of corporatism that all have been justified in giving support to the evil principle that lying is just being part of the process. The better the liar, the greater the success for clandestine Coup operations.

Though the critics of Wokeism outnumber its supporters, the Coup's aggressive propagandists have infiltrated strategic positions throughout society. This serves the purpose of creating the chaos needed to undermine civil discourse and cancel the First Amendment in order to gain support for the building of a utopian Marxist society based on lies and false promises.

The National Security State

Without control of the "national security state" the Coup fails. It was discovered early on that national security policy had to be totally controlled by individuals sympathetic to the Coup's ultimate goals. WWII gave a giant boost to these efforts. The real goals of foreign policy had to be kept secret because the American people would reject their lies and needless killing if they knew the truth about the government's plan to cancel the Constitution and remake America in the image of cultural Marxism. Even before the bombing of Pearl Harbor, FDR was maneuvering the US into the war.

Fake patriotism, promises of safety and peace, and false loyalty to the Constitution and the principles of liberty and prosperity, became the politician's buzz words used to justify their deceitful promises needed to gain public support that would distract from their dangerous authoritarian beliefs that led to a war with Japan.

However, accepting the lies of interventionism paved the way for "compromise" to dominate public discussions on foreign and domestic issues. This was viewed as more "practical" than following the Constitution. This of course avoided the fact that these policies could only be accomplished with the sacrifice of liberty and wealth and required secret planning. Sadly, lying to promote a Coup to cancel America's Republic was never a moral concern for the Coup conspirators. It was just smart politics — and besides, right and wrong for them are unknowable.

This development would serve the interests of those who promoted the National Security Act of 1947, which opened the flood gates to those intent on building an American Empire but who needed policing powers to facilitate their activities. With the dollar becoming the world's reserve currency after WWII, the Coup's effort to destroy the Republic and undermine the benefits of Western Civilization became an American controlled project. Influencing various entities like business, families, labor, the military, education, the MSM, social media, sport organizations, religious groups, Hollywood, corporate entities, government-run medical care, the financial system, and especially the FED and the banking system — plus everyone who got brained-washed by aggressive Wokeism — all contributed to the success of the of the grand Coup by stealth.

As the time went by the champions of the Coup became more easily identifiable, regardless of their fake social posturing in the community with their moral standards deteriorating beyond all beliefs. Their arrogant policies painted themselves as hedonistic, uncultured, uncivilized, and irreligious, with a belief that lies were acceptable to promote "science" if it served their political goals of destroying Western Civilization and America's Republic. Sexual mutilation of children, to experiment with gender changes, by intimidation without parental consent is a repulsive criminal act.

Supporters of the Coup are far outnumbered by those who disagree with them, but these people are frozen in disbelief on how to combat the tragic circumstances we face. The Deep State is fanatical in keeping their plans secret and they have never been underfunded since their corporatism is also a money-making scheme — in spite of their lies regarding concern for the poor. Their game plan has been superb in their effort to infiltrate all the major organizations and finance and coerce or punish them in order to gain their compliance in the Coup's sinister takeover of American society.

The strategy for all was to generate systematic chaos no matter how long it took, by promoting racism, Antifa, Black Lives Matter, white hatred, extreme quotas, class warfare with maldistribution of wealth, open borders, and the vicious curtailment of First Amendment rights by using a combination of illegal government and corporate force. We should be especially aware of those who brag about their devotion to the cult of Wokeism and use it as an economic weapon.

America's wealth, military power, and the financial clout it gained with the tremendous benefits that came with control of the world reserve currency — backed by its huge gold holdings — made it the super-power of the world as a consequence of WWII. It was set to enjoy the benefits and power for the foreseeable future. But like all empires, its day would come.

Wokeism, has become an organized "army" to infiltrate every aspect of American life in order to transform it into something quite different than the Republic it was intended to be. To do that, its proponents must both undermine all the restraints against tyranny placed in the Constitution and demonize the principles in the Declaration of Independence for which the Revolution was fought.

Exposing the criminals who stole Western Civilization and identifying the forces that pulled off The great Surreptitious Coup against America's LIBERTY is the ongoing crucial battle now being fought in our inner cities and in the many foreign lands where the US military maintains and expands our Empire all the while our citizens endure the tragic misfortune of a society plagued with a moral and financial bankruptcy. Knowledge and an understanding of this ordeal is scarce as a result of the education most Americans receive in government schools.

Worldwide, resentment has built over America's determination to control the international financial and political institutions like the UN, NATO, IMF, World Bank, and trade policy. As an Empire we insisted on having a say over international borders and finance, natural resources, and most military activity throughout the world.

The extent of these operations has provided opportunities for profiteering by the military-Industrial complex in the very lucrative weapons industry. It is an arrangement that has provided the funds needed to control and expand their political control over Congress. This terrible result has led to strong bipartisan support for empire-building that included propagandizing for wholesale foreign intervention for increasing political power and huge benefits to the bottom line of the corporate participants.

Sadly, there's no reason to expect that foreign non-interventionism will be seriously considered by either political party. Tinkering with Congressional House rules will not provide competition to the pro-war clout of the military-industrial complex.

The bigger the empire, the greater becomes its need to demand secrecy of its operations, control of the foreign policy, and increase the corrupt wealth associated with it. These efforts have been identified as being managed by "The Deep State." As their operation became better understood and despised, strong resentment developed against it. But the resistors lacked the ability to uproot the scheme and gain enough political support to stop the long-term plans to overthrow our Constitutional government at the expense of Western Civilization.

An explosive wakeup call: November 22, 1963.

The alarm bells are still ringing, loud and clear. The Surreptitious Coup is more easily recognized in 2023 than it was 60 years ago in 1963. Its influence has steadily increased and was achieved by the tomfoolery of Wokeism lies and its partnership with social media, corporatism, investment and financial organizations, the Justice Department, along with a partnership it developed with the "national security state" including the FBI, DHS, and the CIA. This alliance continues to pose a grave danger to American sovereignty and Western Civilization and is more dangerous than the pretend bipartisan agreements in the Congress. November 22, 1963, will prove to be the announcement date of gargantuan historic significance, yet to be recognized to its full measure. And it's already humungous.

On November 21, 1963, as the senior flight surgeon at Kelly Air Force Base in San Antonio, I was asked to "stand by" because President Kennedy was going to be on the Base for a short time. It was basically a courtesy call and I had no specific responsibility related to the President's short visit.

Little did anyone know that an assassination was awaiting that would reveal an ongoing historic and dangerous Coup. It would over time be endlessly studied and made available for the world to analyze. The true significance of the Coup was bound to be exposed and steadily the world would come to realize that Western Civilization and The American Republic were under attack.

The full significance of the November 22, 1963, assassination is yet to be fully understood and what it really means for the Cause of FREEDOM.

Kennedy was dead within 24 hours of my watching Air Force One fly over the Base taking the President to his next brief stop in Houston before flying on to Fort Worth to be ready for his early morning activities in Fort Worth. Before leaving for Dallas, he had breakfast with the local Chamber of Commerce and in his brief comments there, he optimistically stated that, "We are still the keystone in the arch of freedom...." And we need to be "second to none."

It was on Sept 14, 1960, when Kennedy was nearing the end to his successful campaign for President, in a speech at the Waldorf Astoria, he said: "We age fast in this business of running for the greatest office in the free world." He closed with referencing a President Franklin Roosevelt famous phrase; "We have the same rendezvous with destiny that Franklin Roosevelt spoke of about 25 years ago."

Kennedy 's speech for a more peaceful world

Kennedy's outline of his peace plans caught the world's attention in his famous address at the American University in Washington D. C. on June 10, 1963.The leaders of the Coup were listening and they were not pleased. This speech was given five months before November 22,1963. It served to solidify the conspirators' resolve to murder Kennedy. And, from their point of view they had good reason to be concerned. The speech was inspiring and was received much better than most pundits had expected.

In the twelve days of accelerated negotiations after it was given, the Partial Nuclear Test Ban Treaty was signed by Representatives of the Soviet Union, the United Kingdom, and the United States in Moscow on August 5,1963, with ratification by the US Senate on Sept 24,1963 by a vote of 80-19. With Kennedy's signature it became law on October 7, an impressive legislative feat. But it also helped to set the stage for Nov 22. By then, there was no turning back.

Sadly though, Kennedy's call for a more peaceful

world was met by a chorus of outcries from the proponents of needless war, which included especially the participants in the planned Coup that was then targeting the President. Strong evidence has been gathered over the years that the murder was planned by active and retired CIA agents — with Allen Dulles the probable ringleader — along with many others who played a part in the treasonous act. The Deep State was not about to allow peace to break out in the midst of serious planning to solidify and expand their Empire. It became clear to them that Constitutional rights and Western Civilization would need to be sacrificed and downsized. Unfortunately, the grand Coup has continued to succeed in its efforts to undo thousands of years of human progress.

But the final chapter to this ordeal, has not yet been written.

The stakes are high since the fate of Civilization hinges on who wins the philosophic struggle between the nihilists, who deny the existence of "truth," and the proponents of a society based on a higher law that maintains that moral and ethical standards are natural to mankind.

The subtle but horrible plans, gigantic in historic importance, were continued with even greater determination to silence the voices seeking a different approach with the Soviets and world peace as well. The MAD doctrine, for Kennedy, was ingrained with risks that should be avoided. The usual chicken hawks, who were strongly supported by the military-industrial complex, combined their efforts with various other individuals and factions that shared their hatred for Kennedy, with many of them joining the Coup's conspiratorial efforts.

The most bitter enemy of Kennedy, as cited by many historians, was Allen Dulles, a former head of the CIA fired by Kennedy over the Bay of Pigs fiasco. He has been often linked to the assassination in the books written about that tragedy. However, the co-conspirators were many. Even LBJ was said to be aware of the assassination plans.

The decade of the 1960's was a deadly time for the Republic, opening a path for subsequent Wokeist challenges to previously beneficial achievements of Western Civilization under higher law principles.

A recent revelation showed that the best students in many of our government schools, out of fear of hurting other students' feelings, are being denied favorable recognition for academic achievements that they had earned. This gives us a hint as to the intellectual direction the Coup is taking us. Being a "merit scholar" is now being frowned upon rather than recognized and praised.

The result is that the Coup is no longer surreptitious. The "Age of Deceit" has been thrust upon us with an ugly replacement for those seeking the goals of peace, to one of violence in an age of criminal lying. The danger it poses to the Republic and civil discourse should be obvious. The 1960's will be known as the decade when "The New World Order" took over and ushered in "The Age of Deceit" while placing the search for truth in deep hibernation.

The speech that was 'canceled'

The participants in the Coup's plans to murder Kennedy saw fit to do it on his way to Dealey Plaza on November 22, 1963 to give a speech at the Trade Mart in

Dallas. Before this dastardly deed occurred, the Plaza already had its own favorable reputation and was recognized as "The Front Door of Dallas." "It served as the major gateway to the city from the west, equally important, as a symbol of civic pride." The choice may have been a result of political spite and its usefulness in the strategy for framing Oswald as the patsy.

Much of this speech was political cover for Kennedy boosting his support for a strong military defense to offset the impression that he was seen as too willing to seek diplomatic peaceful solutions over saber rattling, as a prelude to his preparation for the presidential election one year off.

This speech was intended to give Kennedy the opportunity to reemphasize his firm beliefs that lower taxes would be helpful to the economy, unlike the policies of the war hawks. This position had already annoyed many and added to those who distrusted Kennedy. His closing comments in his Peace Speech however, revealed his sincere efforts to promote the cause of peace, which in reality was the major reason for his assassination.

A few quotes from "the most famous speech- never given":

"Finally, it should be clear by now that a nation can be no stronger abroad than she is at home. Only an America which practices what it preaches about equal rights and social justice will be respected by those whose choice affects our future."

"That strength will never be used in pursuit of aggressive ambitions-it will always be used in pursuit of peace. It will never be used to promote provocations — it will always be used to promote the peaceful settlement of disputes."

"...therefore, that we may exercise our strength with wisdom and restraint, and that we achieve in our time and for all time the ancient wisdom of 'peace on earth, good will toward men. That must always be our goal, and the righteousness of our cause must always underline our strength."

The aftermath

Anybody that generates the amount of hate from the powerful Deep State that Kennedy did shows that he must have had a great deal of influence and integrity to be seen as a great threat to the entrenched military-Industrial complex and "national security state." The significance of the Coup itself was not immediately understood since the establishment's propogandists influenced millions that the lone gunman, Oswald, was guilty as declared by the CIA and MSM. But it didn't take long for America to wake up and challenge the cover-up reported in the Warren Commission report. Today, a quite a large majority of Americans rejects the official Report, as more and more are becoming aware of the growing dangers we face ever since November 22,1963, when the Deep State Coup flaunted its treasonous act. The combination of the Coup's success in gaining political power along with its more recent alliance with Cultural Marxism and Wokeism, justifies the concerns of many for the continuation of Western Civilization and the existence of the American Republic. We must remember that moral and financial bankruptcy is not something we can ever borrow our way out of!

The coverup and the aftermath

The cover-up started immediately. Two days after the Kennedy assassination, Jack Ruby shot Oswald on national TV. Oswald was who the authorities had conveniently set up to be accused of the murder and he was killed to make sure he would never tell his side of the tragedy.

LBJ, now President one week after the assassination, by Executive Order established the Warren Commission on November 29, 1963. Astoundingly, Allen Dulles was named a member and was the individual most people now believe was the strategist for the assassination. The entire Commission charade was not a joke, it was a farce. It may have been history's greatest Coup, yet the perpetrators were chosen to investigate and monitor the effort to sort out the truth.

It is now recognized that the Warren Commission was a pre-planned cover-up. It was obviously designed to hide the truth, not seek the truth. When the 888-page Commission Report was made public on September 27, 1964, a statement made at that time stated that that we would not "know the truth about the assassination in our lifetime." Sixty years later, both Republican and Democrat Presidents have continuously refused to release the full Warren Report — for our own sake, of course. The cover-up has had a long "lifetime."

The perpetrators of the Coup and the cover-up, with support coming from the Woke "Army," were satisfied that, from their point of view, their violence had been successful, since they now had Civilization and the Republic on the ropes — the precise goal of the conspirators. This represents a dubious measurement of "success," since that questions the moral veracity of those who, out of a desire for vengeance, would go to these extremes to continue a policy of constant war in order to achieve wealth and power.

Jack Ruby's killing of Oswald was only the beginning of the many others who met untimely deaths. It's been estimated that over 100 people associated in some way with the assassination died under suspicious circumstances. Something fishy was going on, even though the details of each case were difficult to assess.

Mary Pinchot Meyers

The most dramatic of these many so-called "coincidental" deaths, was the murder of Mary Pinchot Meyers on October 12, 1964, almost one year after the assassination of President Kennedy. The evidence was overwhelming that the CIA was likely very much involved in this killing. Like in the JFK murder, the CIA had precise plans to frame an innocent person. This time they set up a black man to be in the wrong place at the precise time. The CIA's conspiracy to frame Ray Crump failed when the suspect was surprisingly exonerated at his rigged trial-thanks to a brilliant defense lawyer. This murder is still classified as "an unsolved murder." This sequence of events occurred without public knowledge of the several years-long affair between Kennedy and Mary Meyers. Their relationship has been described as a true love affair and Mary strongly endorsed the President's growing intense desire to promote the cause of peace. Along with their shared devotion to this cause, it is easy to understand the CIA's ugly war with Kennedy. Peace is always a strong deterrent to the immoral wars of tyrants-something that terrifies all authoritarians. This is a good reason for everyone to be vigilant when dealing with the CIA or the FBI.

The special relationship that Mary Meyers had with Kennedy is why she also had to be eliminated. It was assumed, correctly, that she knew too much about the truth of the CIA's involvement in the assassination and could not be trusted to remain silent.

This Coup indeed was thorough and vicious and was meant to have long-term ramifications for the US Empire in world affairs. This was an open declaration that the "national security state," especially including the CIA, was in charge of the Deep State and was now benefitting from Wokeism activists. Chaos is always helpful to authoritarians seeking power. Life in America was about to significantly change with this open declaration of war against the Republic and Western Civilization. They're in charge now and nobody even knows where their home office is located.

The history of the assassination of Jack Kennedy, the effort to cover-up the evil of the CIA with the fake Warren Commission, the murder of Mary Meyers along with the effort to frame an innocent person for it, and the evidence that it was carried out by the CIA arm of the Deep State, reveals a lot, but it begs the question: WHY. What were the goals of those who were so willing to spill so much blood in their treasonous effort to undermine liberty at home and peace abroad?

Progressivism in the first half of the 20th Century set the stage for the domestic part of the Coup to advance its plans for burying the Republic and replacing it with the un-restrained power of "The "national security state"." Teddy Roosevelt, Woodrow Wilson, Franklin Roosevelt, and Harry Truman saw to it that the United States moved into the big leagues of dominating world affairs. Conditions were irresistible: the US was spared the destruction of WWII, the dollar became the reserve currency, our gold holdings were immense, we retained memory of the of how free markets work, and we had the strongest military of all history. Ig-nored was the fact that the philosophic fundamentals that encourage a Republic were being eroded. This was ignored because the wealth was previously earned and deceptive. The economic conditions were favorable for unlimited bor-rowing, but not forever. Now the payment has come due.

The decade of the 1960's showed clear evidence that the Coup was of greater significance than many realized at the time and even bigger than an assassination of a presi-dent. More earth-shattering assassinations were destined to be carried out before the decade ended and combined with the violence surrounding the Robert F. Kennedy and the Martin Luther King murders, the domination of the American political system was rapidly changing and re-flecting the Coup's successful takeover. The violent street protests against the prolonged and useless Vietnam war, along with the deadly war on drugs, demonstrated why Kennedy championed the cause of peace. It was soon recognized that a secret, non-military Coup had taken over the United States government and Western Civilization was under siege. Radical changes were about to occur in the judicial system, the medical system, the military, elections, education system, and in America entire culture by radicalization carried out by Wokeism insanities in alliance with the Cultural Marxists, to bring on the "chaos," they both sought, with plans from which to benefit.

Throughout the 1960's the Coup continued to display its influence, with three major political assassinations that were directly related to the victims' criticism of the US foreign policy of promoting needless war. Funding for the military-Industrial complex has routinely received strong bipartisan approval. The assassinations of Robert F. Kennedy and Matin Luther King were designed to intimidate those who promoted peace by presenting the case for more sensible diplomacy to stop the madness of senseless wars.

An honest assessment of the CIA — something we're lacking — would conclude that the CIA should never have been created. The principle on which it was established is completely foreign to a constitutional republic. The two are incompatible. Its creation was justified by claiming a need for national security protection of our liberty and out of a sense of patriotism. The flaw in this thinking is that freedom can't be secured by sacrificing freedom. Ultimately, one can expect that those secret powers supposedly granted to assure the peoples' safety will eventually be used against its own citizens, not foreign invaders. It's similar to the Federal Reserve, which was created to provide stable prices and full employment for the middle class and instead it turned out protecting the wealth of the rich in the military-Industrial complex, the pharmaceutical industry, and the banking system.

The effort to undermine the culture and wealth that had been created by Western Civilization has continued for centuries by those seeking a system of collectivism while ignoring how the spirit of liberty and natural law played a significant role in its success. This ongoing resistance over the centuries has come from the enemies of civilization who reject spirituality and instead enthusiastically accept the notion that truth is not knowable. Their claim is that the higher law principle should be replaced by accepting government authority or a political party as being all-knowing and the ultimate arbiter of the moral standards of "right and wrong." Radical authoritarians are boastful about their aggressive atheism and nihilistic beliefs that find democracies to be fertile fields for developing by deception a "free stuff" philosophy. The contest between nihilism and natural law is not a 20th Century phenomenon. Governments distributing "stolen goods" for political gain is plunder, not charity, and the process has been around for a long time.

The current battle between nihilism and natural law has existed since the beginning of the 20th century with the arrival of American Progressivism. International support for militant fascism and communism gave us the carnage of WWI, WWII, the Korean War, the Vietnam War, and many other smaller wars.

The struggle has greatly accelerated since the end of WWII. This has involved challenging the cultural and economic wonders of Western Civilization with a desire to also replace the political structure of the United States, but not by the ballot box or philosophical persuasion. Instead, promoting the rotting away of the Bill of Rights has been successful in the evaporation of the Republic by the deadly surreptitious Coup.

This Coup came of age in the 1960's, with an aggressive domestic takeover, not requiring a foreign invasion, that signaled plans for the expansion of the American Empire. The bold and overwhelming success by the key members of the "national security state" ushered in the age of deliberate lying and intimidation by the government at the expense of protecting the Republic.

Sufficient evidence over the years has accumulated that has led to a large percentage of the American people to believe that our own government participated in the murder of prominent politicians who held pro-peace views. Those who boldly speak out for peace continue to be targets of the military-industrial hawks and their fellow-travelers who claim that only they care about national security with a willingness to participate in a Coup and start a war to prove it.

What evolved was a significant shift in power to the CIA and the FBI in an alliance with the "national security state," which together gained an ability to squelch debate, operate in secrecy, and threaten skeptics with economic and social punishment. An efficient operation to carry this out needed a tremendous amount of infiltration into the social, medical, government, and financial organizations by the Woke "Army." It was aided by the religious zeal of influential radical environmentalists, who were pressured to carry out the marching orders of the incognito leaders of the New World Order. The Woke "army" includes the corporatists working with the government to carry out the punishments for disobeying social justice mandates that were intent on sacrificing First Amendment rights. All this, while our moral and financial bankruptcy marched on!

Truman's second thoughts on the CIA

Truman had some second thoughts about the CIA and his particular responsibility for its creation in 1947. On June 6, 1963, five months before his assassination, President Kennedy gave his historic "Peace Speech" at American University in Washington D.C. Just one month after the assassination, Truman wrote an op-ed for the Washington Post with the headline "Limit CIA Role to Intelligence." His argument was that the CIA no longer even pretended to limit its activities to "intelligence collection" and had become "an operational...and a policy-making arm of the Government" in secret. This change in attitude delivered tremendous power to a Coup that had just been identified as a lawless organization. In the 60 years since, the mischief that the CIA has engaged in has subsequently caused many to recognize 1963 as a "crossing the Rubicon" event. The philosophic "Coup," that originated with the Progressive movement at the beginning of the Twentieth Century, made giant steps in solidifying its power by the events of 1963. The steady erosion of America's Republic can only be understood with a recognition of the inexorable increase of CIA power and the influence of the entire national security state's war on the Fourth Amendment.

Taking on the CIA this close to the assassination before there was any significant talk of possible CIA involvement was bold, though Truman, in his op-ed, made an effort to distance himself from supporting something more than "intelligence gathering." Regardless, the National Security Act opened wide the doors to America's efforts to establish an empire, financed by a secretive central bank, and "blessed" with the world's reserve currency backed by tons of gold.

When it came to the "national security state," Truman was far more sensible than "Wild Bill" Donovan, who was the driving force for making the CIA as radical as possible. He lobbied FDR in 1944 for an intelligence agency that could use both covert and overt methods and have authority to conduct "subversive" operations abroad. The die had been cast and the age of the American Coup had begun in earnest. However, this aggressive policy will end when the dollar loses its clout as the world's reserve currency. And that time is now fast approaching.

The Church Committee

The inevitable growth of the secret powers of the CIA and the abusive growth of the entire surveillance state did not occur without some resistance. By 1975 it was discovered that the CIA was involved in the drugging and torture of US citizens in human experiments on mind control. They were also engaged in surveillance and infiltration of political and civil-rights organizations, assassinations of foreign leaders, and systematic interference in foreign and domestic news organizations. Back then, it was fear-mongering over the communist threat, these days it has been Covid hysteria and Chinese balloons.

These revelations were significant and inspired the

establishment of the Church Committee to conduct a thorough investigation. The Committee served a worthy purpose in warning the American people of the grave dangers of unsupervised surveillance. Even though they were already known to be unconstitutional and immoral, the politicians justified the activities by claiming their necessity in order to protect our national security and civil liberties. Sadly, these same excuses are still being used today to undermine our First Amendment rights.

Partners in crime: the FBI and the CIA

The US Senate Select Committee in 1975 exposed the many abuses of the CIA, NSA, FBI, and the IRS. At the time, Seymour Hersh did some great reporting on the CIA's abuses. The Church Committee produced voluminous reports resulting from its very detailed investigations and recommendations. An effort was made to stop all assassinations of foreign leaders and illegal spying on American citizens. The FISA courts were created to prevent unreasonable searches and seizures. All these wonderful promises would instead lead to a collusion between FISA and the FBI in a gigantic political scandal involving the integrity of the election process in recent years.

"Black" prisons have continued to exist, and the world is aware of the torture the CIA has still been involved in since the time the Church Committee "banned torture forever." There have been estimates made that there are 50 secret prisons in 28 countries where it is believed by many that torture is still carried out by the United States. Both political parties claim they oppose political assassinations, but evidence shows otherwise.

During the Obama administration, on October 14, 2011, a 16 year old America citizen, son of Anwar Awlaki, was inadvertently assassinated by the CIA. The actual target was Awlaki himself, who was also an American citizen. Two weeks later the CIA finished the job and assassinated him. No legal process was utilized. If that wasn't enough, six years later, on January 29, 2017, Anwar's eight-year-old daughter was killed in a CIA raid during the Trump administration. Anti-American sentiment from the Middle East should not be a surprise.

On January 3, 2020 a very undiplomatic and needless assassination occurred at the Baghdad, Iraq International airport with the assistance of the CIA. The drone attack was carried out by the US Air Force. The target was Qassemi Soleimani, the Iranian major general who was on his way to meet Iraqi Prime Minister Mahdi. The attack killed a total of 10 people. The assassination had nothing to do with US national security and was just another ill-advised military attack in the decades-old war in the Middle East. The bottom line is: It was an illegal, unconstitutional, immoral, costly attack that made America less safe, poorer, and less free by further promoting our policy of foreign interventionism. It's precisely this policy that is playing a significant role in driving us toward the shattering of our and the world economy.

A renewed effort — will it matter?

There are now calls for a new Church Committee to rein in the Coup's operatives who are now running roughshod over the First and Fourth Amendments. An honest investigation would be worthwhile, but considering the power that the Deep State has gained in recent decades it would be highly unlikely. That considerable power would no-doubt be used to thwart any honest attempt to restore justice to our judicial system. The original Church Committee, even with an honest effort to restore some decency, fizzled rather quickly, and protecting our civil liberties today is much more difficult than it was in the 1970's. The fox is in the hen house and the nihilist rejection of truth runs deeply trough the FBI.

When Dick Cheney was asked about continuing his support for torture as a policy, his answer was swift and disgusting: "I'd do it again in a minute." Forty-five years after the abuses by the NSA, and in particular the CIA, the effort to rein in our government's unconstitutional surveillance on the American people was recognized and condemned, yet conditions are now arguably worse than ever. Truth-tellers are painted as traitors and objective journalists are banned and careers are destroyed. Physicians are being "canceled" and losing their licenses for the audacity of stating the truth about natural immunity.

The Coup is made up of nihilists willing to destroy the reputation of heroic journalists like Seymour Hersh and Julian Assange, along with many others. Truth is anathema to all the authoritarians seeking dictatorial powers. The current members of the Coup that "stole" America's Republic continue with their constant lies to suppress all influence of the principles of natural law. Nihilists are convinced that truth is unknowable. Rejecting truth allows the most aggressive politicians to gain control of the socio-economic order. This distinction separates the supporters of the Coup from those who endorse the Jeffersonian belief that liberty and morality are requirements for a Republic to exist. The evil process that is used to challenge the principles of liberty is Wokeism's systematic attack on reason and "natural law." Their goal is to substitute it with democratic majoritarianism, a fancy description for "the dictatorship of the majority" — a system that is more easily manipulated by political demagogues and wealthy elites who live off the taxpayers.

J. Edgar Hoover was the Director of the FBI for 48 years. His reputation for "law and justice" over the years far exceeded his very controversial "achievements" in law enforcement. To say the least; he was no libertarian and was not restrained by any devotion to the Constitution.

The assassination of Martin Luther King was carried out with CIA and FBI assistance. As part of the Empire, the FBI continued to have an international presence with agents in approximately 75 embassies and consulates around the world. The FBI has a poor record for protecting freedom for American citizens. Illegal surveillance of certain members of Congress and the media was a convenient practice for gathering unflattering evidence that became useful to Hoover when lobbying his case of why he "deserved" to continue his already long career as the super-chief of the national police force.

It should not be a surprise that the FBI in recent years ended up as a "partner" to the Democrat Party with its notorious scandals surrounding "Russiagate" in the 2016 and 2020 elections and Hillary's email scandals. And Hunter Biden's laptop fiasco confirmed a lot about the moral standards of the "Big Guy." The FBI stayed busy rounding up lockdown resisters, including those who merely expressed disagreement with unconstitutional executive orders.

Yes, I do believe that there are some reputable employees of the FBI, but not enough in influential positions for us to trust the Bureau to be a protector of liberty. Our justice system is broken. And without justice, a Republic cannot exist. The longer the likes of Attorney General Merrick Garland remain in charge of the justice system, the longer truth and morality will be "canceled" from our political process. The two are incompatible!

Many recent surveys indicate that an increasing percentage of Americans no longer believe our elections are carried out in a fair manner. There are meager expectations that the 2024 presidential election will provide answers to the tragic conditions created by the "Surreptitious Coup," which for the past 125 years has undermined the human energy that created the astounding wealth of Western Civilization and taken down the American Republic.

There is a better way to go

First, cancel the war against ourselves. Our wounds are self-inflicted, yet we continue to spend trillions of dollars searching for more "monsters to destroy" in order to maintain and expand our empire. Preparing for WWIII has dramatically accelerated in recent years, especially since the European Union, NATO, Ukraine, and the US pulled-off a complete Coup of the democratically elected government of Ukraine in 2014.

The intense public clamor for war preparation utilizes Russia and China as the "current monsters" that we must fear and provoke. The military-Industrial complex and various other special interest groups are cheering on these plans. An early March 2023 nationwide poll showed 43.4 percent of US voters claim that we are "on the brink of WWIII," and imply that it's due to the aggression against us by other nations, especially China. This argument has been wrongly used on many occasions since WWII to justify foolish US militarism around the world.

The odds are that emphasizing our fake need for our foreign adventurism while ignoring the dangers that are involved serves as a distraction from our insidious domestic policies that threaten us and are of our own making. A financial-economic crisis, driven by a $31+ trillion debt now in the process of liquidation through inflation, is a warning that all is not well with the Federal Reserve's effort to miraculously maneuver a "soft-landing." This implies that our leaders believe that paying for the extravagance of the past 50 years is not a critical issue. There is little concern for the Constitution or the risk that our policies will precipitate a domestic war that threatens our liberties. The threat of war is real, but the greater dangers are coming from within. The brewing major war engaging Europe and Asia makes no sense.

There is a legitimate concern for war breaking out, but the warnings that it will resemble WWI and II may miss out in preparing for an entirely different type of an event. The enemies we would likely have to face, and there are many, would make it very difficult for the US to mobilize a military force comparable to what was required in WWII.

The will is not there, the financing is not there, and

world animosity towards the US has grown significantly. In the 1940's, our empire was young and respected. Today its living off its past laurels; unlimited debt; and the consequence of an economic and monetary crisis hatched in 1971 that is only now threatening the world's financial system, spoiled by an unearned confidence in the dollar.

This precarious situation invites retaliation from countries that have suffered from our economic sanctions and military bullying. The American people's support for war is currently decreasing and once the voters realize that foreign wars are a huge drain on our prosperity and make us less secure, they will resist the military state. Corporatism eventually will be seen for the danger it is. Domestic violence, generated by the evil of Wokeism which is already out of control, will force our interventionists to renege on their foolish acts and false promises to our complicit allies who supported the 2014 NATO/US coup of Ukraine that is now being used to ignite WWIII.

An option that ought to be considered

Changing our foreign policy to one that rejects the notion that it is our destiny to own the world's "wealthiest" empire is required. The principle that it is our patriotic duty to protect "our interests" anywhere in the world without defining "our interests" is foolish and dangerous. The growth of the empire was aided by our "ownership" of the world's reserve currency and our military power. Since 1971, with the dollar no longer linked to gold, the fiat currency that replaced it allowed the accumulation of an unpayable 32 trillion-dollar debt that market forces will demand liquidation of.

A foreign policy that conforms with the Constitution should be our guide: No wars without explicit Congressional authority; calling a war a "police action" is not permissible; claiming that authority for war can come from the United Nations or NATO is in defiance of the Constitution. Justifying a war by a Presidential Executive Order makes the President a dictator. After the fact, once a war is illegally initiated, it can still be stopped by a vigilant Congress by not funding it. The problem with this is that the defunding comes after many deaths and huge costs have occurred. Competing with the propagandists is difficult since the profiteering by the military-Industrial complex smothers the warnings by the opponents of the war. Avoiding unconstitutional war is far superior to the death and destruction that occurs before the people demand the politicians stop the useless killing and the abuse of the war authority that served to facilitate the expansion of the American Empire.

The Future of Western Civilization, the Coup of the America Republic, and wokeism influence — A summation

Can Wokeism be stopped? Can respect for Truth be regained? Can America's Republic be restored? Our country is in a quandary and inundated with fear and an epidemic of "acceptable" political lying. A failed economic system operating with a monetary system based on fraud, equivalent to counterfeit, has failed. It is a system wrought with "moral hazards," designed to entice the masses to become dependent on a welfare system that they were promised would serve the rich and poor alike. But instead, the beneficiaries became addicted to a politically dangerous dependency on authoritarianism. This satisfied the Coup's plans to destroy the natural instincts for self-reliance and social cohesion based on free society principles that are necessary for a successful Republic to exist.

A "unit of account" is required

A definable "unit of account" is required in a society that respects self-reliance in economics, social activities, athletics, religion, sexual relationships, and entertainment. Voluntary rules are needed but not arbitrary laws and regulations by government.

A precise "unit of account" used to maintain integrity in all human relations is required, since all human relationships in a free society should have similar goals and purpose.

The monetary unit sets worthwhile guidelines and explains the benefits of precisely defining value in economic calculations. In recent times, dishonesty in "weights and measures" has made economic calculations more difficult. Without a definition of the dollar relating to something of real value, the currency becomes "fiat" (politically defined and arbitrary) and inevitably the economic system ends badly with a financial crisis. Economic calculations are greatly altered when the "unit of account" is not definable. This fallacy makes the true rate of interest and wise economic decisions elusive and promotes recessions, depressions, and price inflation, as well as economic and political chaos.

The absence of truth in defining the monetary unit is economically destructive. And in all other human relationships, a social "unit of account" for decent moral behavior is required to define a higher/natural law for guidance that, if absent, can undermine the benefits gained from past and present Civilizations.

Today, we are witnessing a systematic attack on Western Civilization by many who assume that its greatness should be removed from the pages of history. Though many benefits of civilization started early in recorded history — five thousand years ago — the greatest advancement in civilization has occurred in the last three hundred years. This is a time in which mankind produced once-unimaginable beneficial changes in living conditions for average people. There are many current observers who are now making the case that Western Civilization has reversed its course and no longer automatically enjoys improvement in social, economic, educational, and cultural conditions that advances civilization.

Recent philosophical thinking in these areas have served to cast legitimate doubts about the future of Western Civilization and America's greatness. The guiding principles of those who are dedicated to the destruction of Western Civilization support the principles of a new religion: Wokeism. In just a few decades, this philosophic movement has been able to engulf the world with beliefs that had smoldered for millennia while challenging the very essence of civilization's inexorable and amazing progress. This required personal ingenuity guided by a universal interest in Nature's "higher law." Undermining the principle of "our home is our castle" endorses the notion that only bigots challenge the principle that the "uninvited" have free access to what others have created and own. Homes, fences, and borders have a place in a civilized society. Without this understanding, civilization reverses itself, civil discourse breaks down, private ownership gives into collectivism, and political powers are usurped by the leaders of the Coup.

The enemies of civilization reject the notion that universal truth is worth seeking, since they are convinced that it is unknowable. This nihilistic view is accepted by the leaders of Wokeism who are only too eager to fill the void with their own substitute for truth. And they are not reticent in sacrificing liberty for their obsession with the lies told by the Woke authoritarians.

The evidence is overwhelming that the damage Wokeism has done to the culture of civilization justifies the concerns for its future. The onset of the Coup that took over the American Republic was stamped with approval by the CIA and other members of the "national security state" in the ominous year of 1963. The precise day and place when the conspirators "crossed America's Rubicon" and buried the Republic was November 22, 1963, with the assassination of John Fitzgerald Kennedy in Dealey Square, Dallas.

The coverup, the subsequent assassinations of RFK, MLK, and the deaths of many others who were said to be loosely connected to President Kennedy's murder and knowledgeable about the CIA's participation, soon left the shallow-easy-to-ford-American "Rubicon," far behind, along with Jefferson's dream of an American Republic.

The 1960's were ripe for accepting cultural deterioration, fiscal nonsense, unconstitutional wars, modern monetary theory, and the endorsement of government theft and counterfeiting with out-of-control taxation designed to serve the rich. The seriousness of these policies was ignored in order to pursue the evil Woke course, while the penalties and costs for "stealing" Western Civilization were being delivered to the people who were willing to sacrifice their liberty for short-term benefits. The setback for civilization is not proving to be a national event. It is global in nature and there is no place to hide.

The 1970's did not start with confidence that the Coup was recognizable and that the reaffirmation of the Republic was what we needed. Resistance to the Vietnam war was significant but showed no sign that our pro-war policy was about to change.

The election of 1968 reflected a grassroots disagreement over the Vietnam War with Nixon's large victory by "promising to end the war." Sadly, there was no serious effort on our part for ending the senseless killing in Vietnam until our humiliating surrender and desperate evacuation of Saigon in April 1975. It has been estimated that over 20,000 Americans died in Vietnam after Nixon took over.

It was Nixon's decision to expand the war into Cambodia in April 1970, that led to massive antiwar demonstrations in the US that precipitated the Kent State Massacre on May 4, 1970, which resulted in four students killed and nine wounded. This incident initiated a massive increase in antiwar demonstrations across the US. After the war ended the individuals responsible were identified but there were no significant penalties imposed or changes made in our foreign policy.

No lessons learned

Today the evidence is clear that the FBI participated in the entrapment of innocent bystanders at the January 6 "faked insurrection" at the US Capitol. This political incident has led to probably the worst abuse of our justice system in history. The Coup's successful take-over should be a wake-up call for all Americans. It is now acceptable for the MSM and the Woke politicians to refer to even the most innocent demonstrator as a "domestic terrorist." Only a nihilist could participate in this continuous scheme of attacking and punishing the whistleblowers for telling the truth.

The authoritarian approach to promoting "globalism" in recent decades has made certain that the disintegration of Western Culture will be a worldwide event and not limited to the US. However, a "globalism" guided by the principles of voluntarism and acknowledgement of a higher law, recognizing private property ownership, individual liberty, and a deep respect for truth, would create a decent world order that would be the opposite of the Russia/China "New World Order" which is now being offered to replace the destructive end of the of Western Civilization. This revolution is being led by the new religion of Wokeism that is guided by hate, lies, ignorance, and the nihilist conviction that truth is elusive, making "relative ethics" a seductive tool for those seeking political power.

Evidence abounds with many Woke goals having

successfully infiltrated the Western world, posing grave danger to the future of civilization. Fortunately, a growing number of people are becoming aware of this, but the anti-civilization Coup remains well-entrenched.

Wokeism influence is now affecting almost every social, economic, and political entity — and not in a positive way. Its flowering propaganda claims support for the eradication of racial prejudice and discrimination and social inequalities driven by sexism. These are all code words for identity politics and fake social justice being achieved by guilt-driven policies emphasizing "white privilege" along with a concocted justification for slavery reparations for the weird mystical charge of harm done centuries ago by today's innocent victims who would have to pay for this giveaway. This makes no sense except to those who desire racial strife for evil political gain in the effort to build a Marxist Society on the backs of modern-day slaves. The evidence used to put a guilt trip on current American citizens is the slave trade that started in Virginia in 1619. This occurred 400 years ago and 157 years before Jefferson wrote the Declaration of Independence. Identifying all those truly responsible for this historic event has been found extremely complex and poorly recorded. It is too bad that not even a fraction of time spent on this issue ever deals with modern-day "slavery" that is used to finance the super-wealthy recipients of the largesse that comes from the welfare/warfare state that enslaves the middle class.

The spirit of Wokeism shares an important strategy with its senior Marxist "cousins": All things cultural and economic must first be destroyed to properly rebuild the society as a socialist paradise. It is a dream only a diabolical nihilist could believe in. This is an example of, "saving a system by destroying it." Not exactly a "moral strategy."

There are many consequences of the Coup that quietly and savagely took over the American Republic and institutionalized the authoritarianism of Wokeism. Family and Christian values are under siege; government education has been a huge failure financially and in quality; government education has been deteriorating for decades, but the ill-advised Covid lockdowns have radically accelerated this decline; Critical Race Theory, propagandized as being anti-racist, soon revealed itself as exactly the opposite — racist like Black Lives Matter and Antifa.

These efforts are unfortunately working as desired by those who have the goal of bringing chaos to all things associated with Western Culture. By promoting transgenderism and the obsession with abolishing the use of pronouns and pushing sexual mutilation, radical Wokeist authoritarians claim "diversity" is the only path to an "equitable" distribution of goods and services. This is the exact opposite of seeking equal justice under the law. Following the radical perversion of the justice system, we now witness the tragedy of blindly canceling the Bill of Rights, especially the First and Fourth Amendments. It is safe to say that the government agencies established to protect our natural rights have failed miserably in these efforts and do the opposite. Former House Speake Nancy Pelosi summarizes individual rights as the privilege of the accused to go to court and prove one's innocence. Her evil claim is that a person is guilty until one proves innocence. Just because the IRS follows this gross distortion of the law, it still has no credibility. She also claims that if an act of government has not been explicitly prohibited by the Constitution it is constitutional. Is it any wonder that our country, and especially the judicial system, is in shambles?

This is not a coincidence. Understanding the Coup and how the Wokeist religion took over explains why we should not have been surprised and why we should continue to prepare for bad times ahead.

The culprits behind this preventable tragedy, include the politicians, the bureaucrats, the CIA, the FBI, NSA, the DHS, the IRS, and the Criminal Court System. Not all participants are motivated for the same reasons. The modern-day philosophic Marxists who have dominated our universities for a couple of generations have been the prime movers in the surreptitious Coup that has now forced mankind, once again, to deal with the simple and eternal issue of good vs. evil.

The success of the Coup required the financial assistance from wealthy corporatists who were sympathetic to the plan for abolishing the American Republic and replacing it with the proven failure of another evil authoritarian system.

Is the End of Western Civilization Upon Us?

There have been many warning that Western Civilization is in grave danger and will self-destruct. The warnings emanate from the West, led by the US, as it attempts to deal with its obvious moral and financial bankruptcy with more of the same to come. It may be easy to predict that in the not-distant future, the dethroning of the dollar as the World Reserve currency will occur, but exactly when and how it occurs is unpredictable. A lot will depend on how the "Woke" authoritarians respond with the power they gained by the Coup and how the people react to history's greatest Coup — the takeover of America's once unique Republic and turning it into a "dog eat dog" democracy. The people finally did resist the extreme lockdowns and the lies about Covid, but the government intimidation techniques used are a hint of things to come.

What goes around comes around

Between 1946 and 2000 the United States led the world in foreign interventions and Coups with 81. This policy started early in our history by assuming we had the responsibility of dictating to the Western Hemisphere nations what was best for their national security. Ironically, the Monroe Doctrine in 1823 warned Europeans to cease colonization in the Americas, and the United States promised it "would not interfere in internal European affairs." By the beginning of the 20th century this became a foggy memory.

Three major US Coups played significant roles in ending the American Republic.

1953

In 1953 the US, conspiring with the British government, overthrew the elected Prime Minister Mohammad Mosaddegh and installed Mohammad Reza Pahlavi as the "Shah of Iran." It was all about oil and America's rush to empire. It led to nothing but trouble for the US. It sowed the seeds of radicalism that led to the hostage-taking fiasco in 1979 — from which we still suffer today. As our power and prestige slips away, Iran's coalition now forming with Russia and China should surprise no one. The mistakes we have made with Iran since 1953 are now coming back to haunt us, as Western Civilization and our Republic fades away. Retribution for our Coup-mania is contagious, and we are going to be continually reminded of it. We should not ignore it.

These developments should motivate more Americans to reject the dangerous domestic trends that Wokeism has brought us, and once again consider the magnificence of a Constitutional Republic guided by Nature's higher law.

1961

Eisenhower was President, John Foster Dulles's policies were in vogue as the recent Secretary of State, and Allen Dulles was the Director of the CIA in 1961, the year of The Bay of Pigs. The failed invasion to overthrow Castro occurred on April 17 ,1961. Later that year, on November 29, 1961, President Kennedy fired Allen Dulles. It is this firing that led to a history changing event: the assassination of Kennedy on November 22, 1963.

Immediately, the Coup became apparent to many. Allen Dulles, the probable instigator of this treasonous act, was appointed a member of the Warren Commission, supposedly to find the truth about who murdered Kennedy. However, his real job was to make sure the truth was not revealed. It should not be a surprise to anyone that the justice system in America has continued to deteriorate.

Since 1963, the "national security state" has been used to undermine the liberties of all Americans, except for those that have chosen to participate in the Woke takeover. In the Covid lockdowns "sacrificing a little integrity" could result in financial rewards, keeping your job, and avoiding being "canceled" from society. The changes that came out of the tragedies of the 1960's set the stage for accelerating the deterioration of Western Civilization.

2014

Our participation in the 2014 coup against Ukraine's elected President, Viktor Yanukovych, showed that we are still in the regime-change business. Even while the coup was still going on, our involvement in it became known. The famous transcript of the call between US Assistant Secretary of State, Victoria Nuland and US Ambassador, Geoffrey Pyatt, in early February 2024, revealed it was "coup as usual" for our neocon diplomats. The operation was inappropriately named the "Revolution of Dignity." A better name would have been, "NATO's war against Russia."

The new president, Petro Poroshenko, became president on May 25, 2014, and quickly signed an agreement with the European Union. This agreement satisfied NATO and the US, but disenfranchised the Ukrainians aligned with Russia, especially in Crimea. Surprise: war broke out between NATO-proxy Ukraine and Russia, a war also strongly supported by the US. Under Poroshenko conditions worsened and Poroshenko had not ended the war. This led to Zelensky becoming president — a man who became a good friend of the military-Industrial complex. (Ironically Zelensky ran as the "peace candidate" but soon changed his tune after the election). He was honored by the US Congress with a speech on the House floor to personally lobby for more money and weapons. In the past nine years, the US has spent an obscene $140+ billion on the futile effort of making Ukraine safe for the American empire. The big Coup has already "come around."

Don't worry though: America's bankruptcy and the challenge to the dollar as the world's Reserve Currency will eventually force us to deal with the obsession of protecting the Empire with constant coups. Restoring the Republic is a better option.

Saving Western Civilization

There has been a lot written recently about the end of Western Civilization. Cultural Marxists and other authoritarians are supportive of that goal and strive for it as a way to rebuild society from scratch and establish it as a socialist paradise. Success of this plan is not on the horizon. But we can expect more government intervention in our lives and a continuation of mischief in the economy. This will require a greater effort on our part to promote the only real answer to the social and economic chaos that has been deliberately imposed on us: reject nihilism and accept a higher law principle that includes individual liberty.

There are reasons not to despair over the apparent futility of today's world order. In 1945 despair was set aside in the hope that the end of WWII would bring more peaceful times. August 14, 1945, which I remember well, is identified as VJ Day. The horrifying statistics of the war are mind-boggling. Total deaths are estimated to have been between 35 million and 60 million. The two atomic bombs alone were estimated to have killed over 200,000 people. Though the world has been granted a "reprieve," of sorts, the danger to civilization remains. In the meantime, in the past 78 years, we have not seen the end of Western Civilization. Besides, over-concentrating on "the end of times" can exhaust one's soul.

It is a lonely fight at times, but all civilizations leave a remnant behind to be the guardian of truth, since it will not be found in the morass of typical political infighting for power.

The quiet diligent struggle to understand how best to preserve what is important to aid in civilization's survival usually falls on the few who find the responsibility challenging and personally compelling. Those individuals usually have personal goals of achieving excellence and virtue. An honest effort in sorting out good and evil in context of the higher law, and an awareness of eternal love, serves as an invitation to participate in the remnant. Since the remnant may be represented by a single person or by an amorphous unorganized group, "work" is easy to find. Without a "remnant," the civilization that developed over thousands of years will be threatened with extinction.

Today's arch enemy of a civil society is the evil tool of "Wokeism." This is a secular religion that rejects the moral principles of a higher law that is designed to seek good over evil and truth over nihilism.

Higher law seeks decency and peace through voluntarism and the rejection of aggression. This can only be achieved by recognizing and assuming individual responsibility for all one's actions. This is the essence of all liberty.

Nihilism is the nemesis of liberty, and liberty requires that nihilism be rejected. Truth and nihilism are in an eternal struggle and all nihilists know that to maintain their economic and political power, truth must be silenced. The existence of empires requires constant and expanding lies. Truth becomes treasonous in all empires based on lies. This describes the monstrous political climate in which we live today.

All is not lost. A defeatist who is convinced that it is will be a weak opponent to the Woke revolution. The answer comes by first gaining knowledge of the true nature of Wokeism and its philosophic rejection of truth.

Technology is double-edged. Governments can use it to promote tyranny but those who love liberty and truth can use it to promote peace, tolerance, and prosperity.

Prevailing attitudes of majorities are crucial but that is different than endorsing the political notion that the dictatorship of the majority means it is a good dictatorship. The Founding Fathers were adamant in their warning of the danger of pure democracy which is now a source of the growing dissention in the US. Pure democracy is hard to distinguish from mob rule and when the government gets control of the mainstream media and the social media, majorities can be molded by the propagandists to support unlimited welfare and warfare with debt financing.

But prevailing attitudes, formed by education and common sense of the leaders in a representative republic, will make the difference on whether or not the policies will be accepted. Ultimately the people's attitude makes the difference. The majority of the American people resent the crazy policies of Wokeism, and despite the fact that our political leaders have control of the propaganda machine, eventually reality will prevail. With the right leaders, nihilism will be rejected and the higher law of truth will emerge.

Made in the USA
Monee, IL
09 August 2023

40689957R00052